What Your Parents
*Never Told You About Being a
Mom or Dad*

What Your Parents Never Told You About Being a Mom or Dad

Stan and Jan Berenstain

Crown Publishers, Inc.
New York

Copyright © 1995 by Berenstain Enterprises

Published by Crown Publishers, Inc., 201 East 50th Street, New York, New York 10022. Member of the Crown Publishing Group.

Random House, Inc. New York, Toronto, London, Sydney, Auckland

CROWN is a trademark of Crown Publishers, Inc.

Manufactured in the United States of America

Design by Mercedes Everett

Library of Congress Cataloging-in-Publication Data
Berenstain, Stan,
    What your parents never told you about being a mom or dad / Stan and Jan Berenstain. — 1st ed.
    1. Parenting—Anecdotes. 2. Parenting—Humor. I. Berenstain, Jan. II. title.
    HQ755.8.B47   1995
    649'.1'0207dc20   94-30746
                        CIP

ISBN 0-517-59671-7
10 9 8 7 6 5 4 3 2 1
First Edition

To our wonderful grandchildren
in the order of their appearance:
Sarah, Nora, Sam, and Emily.

Authors' Note

Parenthood is like a bowl of bing cherries—rich, sweet, and occasionally the pits. The reason that no one, heretofore, has revealed its dark secrets should be obvious. If our kids knew what raising kids was really like, we'd never have any grandchildren.

What Your Parents
Never Told You About Being a
Mom or Dad

Introduction

When we were young and twenty (we were twenty-four, actually), we heard a wise man (he was an editor at a New York publishing house, just out of World War II and the Marines, and not much more than twenty-four himself) say, "I've been enjoying your work and it occurs to me that you two might have a book in you." The work he had been enjoying was the back-of-the-book cartoons we were contributing to *The Saturday Evening Post, Collier's,* and other magazines of the day.

As it turned out, we did have a book in us. After some back-and-forthing and some gearing up—we had never written anything longer than a cartoon caption and didn't even own a typewriter—we wrote and illustrated *Berenstain's Baby Book.* The work celebrated and enlarged upon the experience we were immersed in at the time: parenting. We had just become the parents of a splendid baby boy, who is now a splendid middle-aged man, as is his equally splendid younger brother. The soggy, exhausting, around-the-clock experience of feeding, burping, diapering, comforting, and dandling seemed to us to be the stuff of comic catharsis. *Berenstain's Baby Book* did well enough to encourage us to do another book—and another, and another.

The Berenstain Bears came along later (alliteration seems to be our destiny). Now, more than four decades, a hundred books, and four grandchildren later, we have delivered ourselves of another book on that most exciting, inspiring, enriching, exhausting, enervating, and demanding of all human relationships, the parent-child relationship.

As we look back on four decades of parenthood and, more recently, a single decade of grandparenthood, we are bemused to find how little the experience of parenting has changed in some respects, and startled to observe how greatly it has changed in others. New parents must still endure that endless feeding, burping, diapering cycle (though diapers themselves have changed from simple rectangles of moderately absorbent cloth to high-tech prodigies of absorbency capable of containing a flood). Nor have the rewards of being "present at the creation" changed. Newborns are just as miraculous today as they were decades or even centuries ago. Those ten tiny fingers and ten tiny toes are just as astonishing as they ever were. And who is more unchangingly one with the universe than the nursing mother carefully clipping tiny translucent fingernails while her little bee sucks? And it's our guess that incipient moms still discomfit their husbands by deciding to wash their hair after that first premonitory contraction. In the case of the present writers, the spousal response to prepartum hairwashing was something between a fandango and a nervous collapse, to the accompaniment of shouts of "But, honey, the cab will be here any second!" (That's right; we were carless as well as typewriterless.) New moms are still fiercely protective of every aspect of their babies' health, welfare, and comfort. New dads will still move Heaven, Earth, and furniture to accommodate new moms' wishes and whims, perhaps even more so today with so many husbands accompanying their wives into the delivery room to participate in the birthing process. There's no more effective way to demonstrate the unfair distribution of labor in the baby-making process than for hubby to watch his baby being born.

Yes, husbandly hand-holding no longer stops at the delivery room door, as it did in our day. But even without the consciousness-raising delivery room experience, males recognize the moral superiority of motherhood. They understand that theirs is not to reason why, theirs is but to brave the blizzard and procure the pickles for pregnant Mom-To-Be, and after the blessed event, to perform any task Mom may require.

And it was ever thus.

Hark back with us to yesteryear when we were living in a walk-up railroad flat over an Army-Navy store in southwest Philadelphia. As it happened, the flat was directly across from the very factory where Jan had been an aircraft riveter while Stan was away in the Army. It was the summer of '48. An oppressive heat had descended on southwest Philly like a wet shroud. Outside, it was merely sweltering. Inside the flat, it was hotter than the plates that waiters warn you about. It was hotter than the passenger compartment of a New York taxicab in August. Bugs were beating at the paint-stuck windows trying to get out. Sweat fogged our vision. The tar roof of the restaurant next door shimmered in the superheated air. New Dad was working in the front of the flat in the studio/living room that overlooked the street on which four screeching, squealing trolley routes converged. (At night the overhead power poles sparked and crackled like Fourth of July fireworks.) New Mom summoned New Dad to the baby's room where their two-month-old was sleeping fitfully. "This heat," she said, her eyes sparking and crackling like Fourth of July fireworks, "is not good for the baby!"

"But the fan," offered Dad, indicating the large electric swivel fan that was wafting hot air in the direction of the baby, who lay somnolent and sweaty in his crib.

"The fan is not doing the job!" said New Mom. "You've go to do something!"

New Dad scoured his memory bank and with a resourcefulness born of desperation remembered having read that in the heat of ancient Rome, Nero or Caligula or somebody had ordered snow and ice fetched from the mountains. It was then placed in loosely woven hanging baskets and fanned by slaves. A plan began to form in New Dad's fevered brain. "I will," he said, "make an air conditioner to cool the baby!"

"You'll what?" said New Mom.

But Dad was down the walk-up and heading up the busy store-lined street. Past the beer-smelling corner tappy he went; past Centralla's live chicken store; past the air-cooled movie house where *Blood on the Moon*, starring Robert Mitchum, Robert Preston, and Barbara Bel Geddes, was playing; past Richmond's rug and carpet store, where we'd bought the carpet that dissolved when the cat peed on it; all the way to Woolworth's.

"Hair nets?" Dad inquired of the sundries clerk.

"What color?" she asked, pointing to the hair nets.

"Doesn't matter," said New Dad. He paid for a handful of them and headed back down the street. Past the carpet store he went, past the movie house, past the live chicken store, past the tappy, back up the walk-up, and into the baby's sweltering room.

"What do you mean, you're going to make an air conditioner?" demanded New Mom.

"Get me all the ice cubes out of the refrigerator!"

"But those are hair nets. What are you doing with hair nets?"

By the time New Mom had wrestled the encrusted ice cubes out of the hoarfrosted trays and returned with them, Dad had tied the hair nets together and strung them across the room.

"But . . . but . . ." sputtered New Mom.

"It's very simple," Dad explained. "What is an air conditioner but a mechanism consisting of a blower and a refrigerant? Our blower is the fan and our refrigerant is the ice cubes, which I now distribute, thusly, in these little hair net hammocks. All that's needed now," he continued, "is to switch on the fan, thusly, and . . ." BLOOEY! The whole Rube Goldbergian contraption broke loose.

The ice cubes and a shower of ice water flew into the crib onto the baby. New Mom picked up the screaming baby and was about to express herself on the subject of improvised air conditioners. But instead she began to laugh. Soon they were both laughing, at first quietly, then uncontrollably and uproariously. The baby was so distracted, he stopped crying.

And it *was* cooler.

Later that summer we became the first kids on our block to get a new, just introduced, postwar consumer product: a room air conditioner. It cost dearly, and it dripped profusely on the patrons of the Army-Navy store below. But it was truly wonderful. We all moved into the studio/living room for the summer. Even the cat loved it.

A lot more than the advent of room air conditioners has happened since the summer of '48, when we first took on the responsibility of parenthood. The whole baby boom happened. Then the boomers had babies. And now the boomers' babies are having babies. Television, drug wars, and teen sex have happened.

Change has happened.

Television used to be test patterns occasionally interrupted by such programs as "Hopalong Cassidy" and "Howdy Doody." Today television is MTV, VHI, and "Beavis and Butthead," occasionally interrupted by potato chips. Telling your kids about sex used to be a matter of whether. Today it's a matter of how soon and how much. Teenagers used to hang out at Ed's Sugar Bowl, where the worst trouble they could get into was to get caught prying the glass off the pinball machine and jimmying the score. Today's teens hang out at the mall or the convenience store, where the worst trouble they can get into can require lawyers and bailbondsmen.

What's a parent to do? The same thing conscientious parents have always done—their best and their damnedest. In the case of the television, the constitutionally correct, if disingenuous, advice of the television moguls themselves is right on target: what your kids watch on television is *your* responsibility. Ditto with respect to where your children hang out and what they ingest, imbibe, or inhale.

But don't be discouraged. Some changes have been for the better. Take grandparents, for instance. Grandparents used to be pretty awful. At least that's what it said in that first parenting book we wrote more than forty years ago. According to the chapter on the subject (titled "The Grandparent Problem," mind you), grandparents were interfering, schedule-busting, gratuitous-advice-giving, run-amuck baby spoilers. It's different now. Grandparents have improved greatly. They are a whole different kettle of kin. Today's grandparents are, almost without exception, thoughtful, considerate, circumspect, non-interfering paragons of wisdom and generosity.

It is truly remarkable how greatly grandparents have improved over the years. Is it possible that, having become grandparents ourselves, it is our own *perspective* on grandparents that has changed?

It's possible.

The Way It Is Now

A couple of friends of ours occasionally take their six-year-old granddaughter, Lindsey, to what she calls "the fancy restaurant" for Sunday dinner. The restaurant is not so much "fancy" as it is quiet and comfortable, and our friends are regulars there. Being regulars, they have gotten to know the personnel—particularly a young waitress who usually has their table. Particularly enough, in fact, to have seen her through a recent pregnancy, following which they were allowed to see pictures of a marvelously cute baby.

It was shortly after that that our friends took Lindsey, whose own mother was then pregnant, to "the fancy restaurant" for dinner.

Their practice was to show up about five—after all, Lindsey was only six and Monday was a school day—before very many other diners arrived. After ordering drinks—a peppery California Riesling for the grandparents, a Shirley Temple for Lindsey—it was our friends' pleasure to sit and glow with pride in the presence of their beautiful and composed granddaughter. When Beth, the recently pregnant waitress, brought and served their drinks, Granddad introduced Beth to Lindsey.

"Beth, this is Lindsey. You may be interested, Lindsey, in knowing that Beth became a mommy not long ago."

Lindsey *was* interested.

"My mommy's pregnant right now," she said.

"Oh," said Beth. "Do they know yet whether it's going to be a boy or a girl?"

"Well-l-l," said Lindsey. "They're really not sure. You see, when they did the ultrasound the foot was in the way."

Beth went wide-eyed, smiled fixedly, and retreated to the

kitchen. Our friends slugged their wine and Lindsey sipped her Shirley Temple.

The Only Thing
for Sure Is Change

We're not talking about anything so trifling as social, cultural, or political change. We're talking about diapers. We're talking about revolutionary, epoch-making change—namely, the change in diaper technology which has occurred over the last three generations. The invention of superabsorbent disposable diapers—Pampers, Luvs, Huggies, and the rest—has been at least as important to the parenting industry as the development of computer technology has been to all other industries.

In our day, diapers were neither superabsorbent nor disposable. Diapers were big squares of cloth that were either owned—about three dozen was a normal complement—or rented from the Cascade (or similarly named) Diaper Service. The endless cycle of changing, john sloshing, and either washing or stowing diapers in the diaper service can cast a pungent pall over entire households. One has only to recall that tall, cylindrical diaper can standing in the bathroom, the ammoniac exudations of its contents fighting furiously with the sinus-clearing effusions of the deodorant cake trapped in its lid, to know what a difference disposables have made.

And let's not forget another important diaper advance—that great and merciful thumb saver, sticky tapes. When it came to diapering, the nondistaff member of our team was not so much all thumbs as all sore thumbs. By the time dads of yore learned to gauge just how much pressure was needed to push the business end of the safety pin through the layers of cloth without getting too much thumb, the diaperee was usually toilet trained.

Toilet training! Another fine mess we used to get into! Diaper management was such a chore that getting the kid out of them was a consummation so desperately to be wished for that it probably accounts for our having raised a whole generation of anal retentives.

It's different now. Pampers, Luvs, and Huggies have transformed toilet training from an if-at-first-you-don't-succeed continuous crisis to a relatively relaxed process.

It all takes some getting used to.

High-tech disposables are so prodigiously absorbent that cotemporary two-year-olds often look like they're wearing Lindbergh-era parchutes. There are minor as well as major advantages. The weight of high-absorbency disposables stabilizes the gait of wobbly walkers by lowering their center of gravity. They also serve as a built-in hassock should the center of gravity not be lowered quite enough.

Is there a significant downside to the prodigious upside to disposables?

You bet there is.

Flash forward with us as we find ourselves in a spaceship hurtling through deep space. We are approaching a strange planet. Our pilot—a Charleton Heston look-alike—avoids atmospheric burn-up by cleverly passing through a hole in the ozone layer. As we hurtle downward at warp speed, we see a familiar face—no, a *familiar head.* It is the spiked head of Lady Liberty. And she is buried up to her neck in a deep endless blanket of something. Something gray. Something non-biodegradable. We come to realize that we are returning to Earth. But it is not the Planet of the Apes. It is the Planet of the Disposables.

Smelly old-fashioned diapers, anyone?

Parenthood

A brief skit performed by Sid Caesar and Carl Reiner on Max Liebman's classic "Your Show of Shows" in the fifties came close to saying it all.

OPEN ON: Sid and Carl gazing proudly at their newborns (off screen) through the nursery window.

SID (transported with joy): There's nothing like 'em.

CARL (also transported, but with a caveat): Yes, but they're a lot of trouble.

SID (maintaining his position): But there's nothing like 'em.

CARL (maintaining *his* position): Yes, but they're a lot of trouble.

Sid and Carl repeat above sequence of lines until . . .
Fade Out.

The End

What To Do About A Colicky Baby Who Simply Will Not Sleep at Night

1. Learn to sleep standing up. Any number of lower animals can do it—and assuredly there's no lower animal than the parent of a colicky baby who simply won't sleep at night.

2. Prepare a mantra of curses and profanity to be intoned when you are waked from a sound sleep by the Cry of the Colicky Baby. It will save you the stress of having to think on your back.

3. Call your pediatrician at all hours (if you don't sleep, *nobody* sleeps!).

4. Adopt a belief in the transmigration of souls and accept your fate as the parent of a colicky baby as just retribution for some absolutely dreadful thing you may have done in an earlier life.

5. Use earplugs (you'll hate yourself in the morning, but, *oh, those Z's!*).

Short Takes I

Never — In response to some behavioral problem presented to him via phone by a distraught mom, a pediatrician we know told the mom that it was just a stage the youngster was going through.

"Doctor," said the mom, after a brief pause, "when do they get to a stage when there aren't any more stages?"

"Mine," said the doc, "are twenty-three, twenty-seven, and thirty-four, and as far as I've been able to determine, the answer is never."

Nobody Does —At some point of high dudgeon and stress your teen will almost certainly resort to that ancient *cri de coeur* "I didn't ask to be born!"

For the sake of keeping on keeping on, resist the temptation to point out that he or she shares the condition of not having solicited existence with exactly every other single living soul on earth.

There's These Great Shoes, Dad, All the Guys Have Them— It may be the case that you can't know what it's like to be somebody else until you've walked in the other fellow's shoes. But if the cost of those $130 Insta-Pump Reeboks came out of your pocket, at least you know how much it *costs* to walk in the other fellow's shoes. .

On Formulating Enforceable Rules for the Care, Management, and Safety of Children

1. *Keep 'em Simple* — Since the enforceability of rules varies inversely with their complexity, stone-ax simplicity should be your goal. *"Don't . . . jump . . . on . . . the . . . bed!!!"* for example, is a much better bet than "Please, sweetie, Mommy would much rather you didn't jump on the bed. It's dangerous and you might get hurt and then Mommy would be sad."

Note: There is always the option of building the punishment into the rule, as in, "Don't jump on the bed or I'll knock your block off!" But that, as in so many things in life, is a matter of personal style.

2. *Keep 'em Few* — A small number of tightly written rules is infinitely easier to enforce than a multiplicity of same. The traffic code, for example, which fits into that little book they give you when you take your driving test, is an administrative piece of cake compared to the tax code, which fills a whole library.

3. *Keep 'em Negative* — Negatively stated rules are more effective than positively stated ones. *"Don't . . . go . . . in . . . the . . . street!!"* for example, is more memorable and persuasive than "Please play in the driveway where it's safe, sweetie." Also avoid modifications and exceptions, such as "Please play in the driveway, sweetie, *unless Mommy or Daddy is watching.*"

Or, to reorder the old song: "Accentuate the negative,

eliminate the positive, and don't mess with Mr. In-Between."

4. *Keep 'em Credible* — Since nothing is more delicate and crumbly than parental credibility, don't lay down any rules you are not prepared to enforce. Thus, "If you don't pick up this stuff, I'm going to throw it in the trash" is unlikely to be effective because any three-year-old worth his materialistic salt knows you're not going to throw away seventy-nine dollars worth of Legos. Whereas, "If you don't pick up this stuff, I'm going to put it up in the attic for a month!" might be persuasive.

Why Is It That . . .

. . . children never want to get into the tub, but once they're in, it takes a wet soapy tantrum to get them out?

The Monster in the Closet and Other Fears—A Checklist

With "spooky stuff" having become so pervasive a part of our entertainment culture, it's inevitable that you are going to have to put in occasional night duty as your child's personal exorcist. And while you have no obligation to become a full-fledged phenomenologist, it would be well to think a bit about how you will deal with your youngster's concerns about ghosts, goblins, and monsters.

Here are some thoughts and ideas for your consideration.

1. *Get an Early Fix on Your Child's Sensitivity to "Spooky Stuff"*— Kids are just as different in their susceptibility to imaginary fears as they are in other ways. Some infants are spooked by anybody less familiar than Mama, while others gleefully call every man "Dada." Assess your child's ability to deal with stories and TV shows in which threat, menace, and conflict figure. If the likes of the Big Bad Wolf and the troll from "The Three Billy Goats Gruff" spook your very young child, back off to less formidable material for a while—for your own sake as well as your child's. It doesn't take much imagination to figure out that if you let an oversusceptible youngster watch "Horror Theater," you're going to end up sleeping three in a bed.

2. *If a Child Is Afraid of the Dark, Try Leaving the Lights on* — It's astonishing how many parents decide to make the lights-off/lights-on question a "battle" issue. A child will fight you on any ground you choose—and will usually win.

If a child is going through a difficult "night fears" period, leaving the lights on for a few nights won't destroy your parental authority. A three-way bulb or rheostat lamp unceremoniously dimmed each night will usually help work through the problem. A friendly night-light or a light left on in the hall are other obvious expedients. Most kids, if you give them half a chance, will eventually get bored with imaginary fears.

3. *The Monster in the Closet is Imaginary, but the Fear Is Real* — Telling a frightened youngster that the monster in his closet "is all in his imagination" is about as helpful as telling a migraine sufferer that it's all in his head. This sort of fear is best dealt with through friendly but matter-of-fact demonstrations of the vacant nature of the closet—plus some kindly distraction: warm milk (no cookies, please; it mustn't get to be too much fun) and perhaps an extra teddy or two to sleep with.

4. *Some Children Are Able to Work out Their Fears Through Creative Play* — Does the wicked witch in *Snow White* give your child fits? Get out the Magic Markers and the giant scribble pad and encourage Junior to draw some weird, wild, wonderful witches. React enthusiastically: "That's a wonderful witch, sweetie—I especially like that big wart on her chin. And that long curly hair growing out of it is pure poetry!" Ditto with modeling clay. And with modeling clay you have the additional advantage of being able to bash the wicked thing into an amorphous lump after you've had your way with her.

5. *Some Kids Really Do Love Monsters and Such and Thrive on Them* — Some youngsters just love the whole idea of ghosts, monsters, spooks, and all kinds of things that go bump in the night. Sometimes it is a child's way of dealing with fears, but as often as not it is just a harmless, even mindless, preoccupation. Just as some kids are dinosaur crazy or Barbie happy, others are monster mad, and as long as it doesn't give *you* nightmares, it is probably nothing to worry about.

Zen and the Art of Answering Unanswerable Questions

One of the things our parents never told *us* about being a mom or dad was that children, even very young children, are capable of coming up with some pretty fancy insights—occasionally even answers to questions that have stumped the experts for ages.

Some time ago, when interest in Eastern religions was in the air, a young father we know took the following question from his son, Steve, who was ten: "Dad, my World Cultures teacher, Mr. Foley, said how there's all these different religions in the world, and he said there was a Japanese one called Zen. What's Zen?"

The young father lowered the newspaper he had been reading, looked off into the distance, and took his best shot.

"Zen," he said, "is sort of a philosophical religion. It is dedicated, as are most of the world's religions, to seeking perfect truth and wisdom."

Steve's five-year-old brother, Robert, who had been on the floor playing with his Hot Wheels collection, came over to listen.

"The means by which Zen Masters seek truth," Dad continued, "is the asking of unanswerable questions."

"Unanswerable questions," mused Steve. "What *sort* of unanswerable questions?"

Dad was ready with the only one he knew. "Here's the best-known one: What is the sound of one hand clapping?" Dad was pleased to see that son Steven was properly impressed with old Dad's expertise.

Son Robert was not so impressed. The unanswerable question was hardly out of Dad's mouth when five-year-old Robert raised a hand, palm forward, fingers together, and by striking his fingers against the heel of the same hand produced . . .

. . . the sound of one hand clapping.

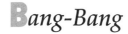

Bang-Bang

While granting that the nature versus nurture argument may never be fully settled, we submit the following:

The parents of a little boy were bound and determined to shut off their son from the influence of guns. They not only saw to it that he was not exposed to toy guns, they rigorously supervised his TV and video watching. He was allowed no cowboy pictures, no "violent" cartoons, no space operas, no anything that showed characters indulging in any activity remotely resembling gunplay.

Then, to the eternal dismay and puzzlement of his parents, one day when he was about two and a half, he started shooting people with a banana.

Why Is It That . . .

. . . Little League often brings out the best in kids, but more often than is comfortable brings out the worst in their parents?

Sleep No More, Emily Hath Murdered Sleep

Emily, a two-and-a-half-year-old with the charm of a Kewpie doll and the sangfroid of a Goldilocks, is the youngest of the three children of a genial couple who live out on Conestoga Road. Emily is a bright, funny, hard-playing youngster whose sunny smile is such that she is instantly the object of much grandmotherly attention at the local supermarket. Though spirited, Emily is a reasonably cooperative and manageable child—reasonably cooperative, that is, until shadows begin to creep and her body clock tells her that pretty soon her mommy or daddy is going to come and get her and try to put her to bed.

As the witching hour approaches, Emily becomes wary, hyperalert. It doesn't matter what tactics Emily's parents employ—gentle persuasion, subterfuge, or a sudden swooping action—at the first sign that bed is in the offing, all hell breaks loose. What takes place is reminiscent of that endlessly repeated scene in the syndicated TV show "Cops," in which a number of police officers try to put an alleged perpetrator into the back of a police car, all to the accompaniment of the song lyric, "Whatcha gonna do when they come for you? . . ." What Emily's "gonna do" is transform herself from a charming, reasonably manageable child into a kicking, screaming, many-appendaged, Shiva-like, bannister-grabbing creature who not only has the strength of ten, but still has it *at* ten. P.M., that is. Also eleven, twelve, one (as the night passes into the great A.M., a bone-chilling sense of hopelessness fills her parents' beings), two, three, four . . . But, hold! The antiwitching hour approaches. The horizon shows pink. The sun, red-faced with embarrassment at having stayed out so late, begins to edge into view—and Emily becomes her sweet, sunny, charming, reasonably manageable self again.

Breakfast, anyone?

The Three Most Insurmountable Obstacles to Intelligent, Rational Parental Decision Making

1. EXHAUSTION FROM LACK OF SUFFICIENT SLEEP.
2. EXHAUSTION FROM LACK OF SUFFICIENT SLEEP.
3. EXHAUSTION FROM LACK OF SUFFICIENT SLEEP.

Short Takes II

Reel Wisdom — Persuading a child to do it "your way" is like landing a ten-pound bass on a one-pound line—it has to be done very carefully. A firm steady pull rather than a series of tugs and jerks is much more likely to meet with success.

No Contest — Recognize that in any contest with your child you are seriously overmatched. Your child is naturally possessed of the guile of Wile E. Coyote, combined with the sheer energy of the Road Runner, while you, poor soul, are the non-animated equivalent of Elmer Fudd.

Temper! Temper! — A good alternative to counting ten is to remind yourself that it won't be long before your poor timorous beastie of a miscreant child is bigger and stronger than you and may decide to hit you back.

On the Natural Superiority of Children to Dogs and Cats — A dog gives you perfect love, a cat total rejection. A child offers the advantage of giving you perfect love and total rejection—often simultaneously.

The Urge for Grandchildren — Recognize that the parent-child relationship is intrinsically unfair and designed by nature to be so. Lear's crybaby complaint, "How sharper than a serpent's tooth it is/To have a thankless child!" is great poetry but naive commentary. What did the old coot expect? One of the reasons we are so eager for grandchildren is our wish to see our progeny "get theirs."

Get Mad, Don't Get Even — The reverse of the above sentiment has become the conventional wisdom in certain social, political, and business circles, but is poisonous in the family circle. Anger expressed (always within limits) is far less likely to be damaging to self and others than anger harbored for purposes of "getting yours back."

Why
Is It That . . .

. . . kids can remember every single solitary scatological, profane, and sexual thing they hear in the schoolyard, but can't remember the multiplication table?

What Makes Us Do It?

The experience of becoming a parent is akin to going to boot camp and becoming a marine. The Marine Corps's harsh approach to creating a marine involves reducing the candidate to a state of nullity through a series of tests and torments: forced marches with full field pack, obstacle courses, lack of privacy, and grievous indignities—all administered by the proverbial gunny sergeant from hell. Then, having achieved the desired level of degradation, the corps sets about rebuilding the individual into a fierce and purposeful fighting marine.

So it is with becoming a parent. The system of torment is almost a match. Equate the forced march with full field pack with walking the floor toting twenty-five pounds of sleepless kid, the obstacle course with trying to shop with Junior riding your foot or hanging from your dislocated shoulder, the lack of privacy with Junior's compulsion to intrude unannounced on your toilette, the grievous indignities with getting peed and puked upon.

As in the Marine Corps process, it's all designed to reduce the candidate to a nullity, so that the individual can then be rebuilt into a fierce and purposeful parenting machine.

Why do we stand for it? What makes parents do the things they do? What makes parents willingly and relatively uncomplainingly trek from one out-of-stock Toys-"R"-Us to another at Christmas time in search of some terrible toy Junior saw on "Darkwing Duck?" What makes parents accept with grace and equanimity the onerous job of waste management? What makes parents willing and able to read *Curious George Goes to the Hospital* (or even one of our own books) seventy-four bedtimes in a row without going over the edge?

What makes parents do all sorts of mad torturous things—like taking their kids to the zoo, to the science museum, to the art museum? *The art museum?*

And there's no gunny sergeant with the power of life, death, and weekend passes to compel performance. So what makes us do it?

It has long seemed to us that becoming a parent changes you in some deep, essential, nonvolitional way. To the extent that we've thought about it, we've supposed that, as the song has it, "Love Is the Answer." Love, the miracle of birth, those ten tiny fingers and ten tiny toes and that aura of helplessness and vulnerability trailing clouds and glory that comes with each baby. But as it turns out, it's none of those things.

What makes us do it, what makes us undergo the tortures of the damned for the sake of our children, is *chemicals.*

At least that's what it said in the *Times (New York Times,* 2 Nov. 1993 Science Times section). Various scientists around the world, but principally in the United States (the home, please note, of Toys-"R"-Us), began wondering why parents do the things they do. Noticing that prairie voles are not only monogamous but are also excellent parents, they decided to investigate *why* these cuddly little orange rodents were such dedicated parents. They discovered that it was chemicals that made them do it. The research revealed that two hormones, oxytocin and vasopressin—one for the moms and one for the dads—are what pulled the little vole bachelors and bachelorettes away from the singles scene and turned them into conscientious parents. Both hormones have long been known to have a number of functions: oxytocin triggers uterine contractions, vasopressin stimulates protective behavior in mated males. What is new is the knowledge of the effect of these hormones on parental behavior. The results of the research were pretty clear. For example, when vasopressin was blocked in an exemplary vole dad, he not only turned into a lousy parent, but started hanging around bars and reading *Playboy* magazine.

Granted, it's a long reach from prairie voles to human moms and dads. But the reach of science is getting longer and longer. It won't surprise us in the least if it turns out that oxytocin and vasopressin work on us exactly the same way they work on prairie voles.

We kind of like the idea.

It's sort of comforting to think there's a bred-in-the-bone excuse for some of the mad, headlong things we have done for the sake of our kids.

The excuse: We just couldn't help it.

Responding to Children's Artwork

There's a right way and a wrong way to respond to a small child's artwork.

The right way: Examine the work carefully and say something like, "What an interesting painting! Do you want to tell me about it?" If you have a good relationship with the child and strike the right tone, the child may deign to inform you that "it's a pitcher of twelve giraffes skipping rope in a snowstorm."

The wrong way: Look at the work and say, "What a great picture of a big red truck!" You'll know you've put your foot in it when, with teary eye and trembling lip, the artists says, "It's . . . it's . . . it's twelve giraffes skipping rope in a snow-storm."

Bully for Timothy

The besmocked members of Ms. Melchionne's nursery school class are doing one of their favorite things. They are standing in front of their child-size easels creating art.

Small spindly Timothy appears to be emulating Mondrian—but, no, it must be an out-of-kilter tic-tac-toe grid he's creating. At least that's what his application of squiggly X's and O's suggests.

At the next easel stands Jeffrey, a much larger child who is vigorously having at a work that looks like a cross between a de Kooning and a serious accident. Feeling the need for a better brush (his own has been action-painted down to a stump), he unceremoniously reaches out and grabs Timothy's brush right out of his hand. Timothy yells and screams. He tries unsuccessfully to retrieve his brush from Jeffrey. Ms. Melchionne comes a-running with a replacement brush for Timothy.

"You musn't be upset, dear," she explains, "Jeffrey is just trying to express himself."

"Yeah," says Timothy, accepting the replacement brush, "well, why doesn't he express himself on somebody his own size?"

How To Teach Your Children About Sex Without Making a Complete Fool of Yourself

It's a dirty job, but somebody's got to do it. Recognize the fact that if you don't, somebody else will. The way things are going, virtually everybody else will. So unless you're willing to let the likes of Madonna, Howard Stern, and MTV teach your kids about sex, you'd better prepare to do the job yourself.

Will you have difficulty doing it? Probably. Will the stutter you thought you'd overcome reassert itself? Possibly. Will there be moments of truth when your youngster will fix you with a basilisk eye and nail you with tough questions? Sample tough question: "Look, Mom, I understand about how the mommy has an egg and the daddy has a seed and how they make a baby in the mommy's tummy. But what I want to know is how the daddy's seed gets into the mommy's tummy in the first place." *Count* on tough questions.

One of Mark Twain's many contributions to Roget was on the subject of weather. "Everybody talks about the weather," said Twain, "but nobody does anything about it." With sex it's quite the other way: Not everybody talks about sex, but everybody does something about it. Including your kids. So there's little time to lose. Here are some thoughts and ideas that may help you get on with the job.

Coming to Terms with Terms — Introduce correct anatomical terms fairly early. Nothing gets old more quickly than cutesy body-part names. While it's natural enough to hark back to the baby terms of your own childhood when your kids are very young, it's usually a good idea to dispense with them as soon as you are able to come to terms with the proper terms.

It's difficult enough to talk about sex with kids, especially as they grow older, without having to resort to idiotic diminutives for parts that are no longer diminutive. To the parent who anticipates having a problem saying words like *penis, vagina,* and *scrotum,* we offer the same advice a New Yorker gave an out-of-towner who asked how to get to Carnegie Hall. The advice: *Practice!* In front of a mirror, if necessary. Try not to get caught at it, though.

KISS (Keep It Simple, Stupid) — Teaching kids about sex is also fraught with peril in the other direction: the direction of long, overly detailed explanations studded with words like *fallopian, spermatozoon,* and *epididymis.* (You might want to check the last out on your own, though. It's a heckuva mechanism.) Kids' questions about sex should be answered in a straightforward, informative, calm, and age-appropriate manner. It should be borne in mind that until they are about five, kids have no idea that their sexual questions are loaded. They are merely part of the general run of questions kids ask. Do thousand-leggers have a thousand legs? (Not really—thirty is the correct answer.) Why is the sun

WHAT'S DESE?

red when it comes up in the morning? (It is being viewed through the distorting lens of the earth's atmosphere.) Or, as the four-year-old who discovered while in the bath that two marble-like objects had descended into that down-under pouch, asked, "What's dese?" The four-year-old's mother, who had just taken the cap off the "no more tears" shampoo, became preternaturally calm.

"Oh, dose—er, those?" she said. "Sweetie, I'll be back in half a minute."

So, confident that Junior couldn't drown in two inches of water in half a minute, she tore out to the studio where Daddy was working on a *Collier's* cover (it was long before we started doing our bears). She filled Daddy in on the way back to the bathroom, giving him mere seconds to formulate an answer. Here, for what it's worth, is how he answered Junior's question: "Well, son, those are glands. We have lots of different kinds of glands in our bodies. Those glands are the ones that make you a boy. They're called testicles. Girls have glands, too—ones that make girls girls. They have a different name and they're inside their bodies."

The four-year-old listened politely and had no comment. "Well," said Mommy. "Your daddy has to get back to work, and we'd better do your shampoo if we're going to get done in time for 'The Three Stooges.'"

It's Different Now — When Hector and we were pups and fear of pregnancy was enough to keep the sexual revolution at bay, most pubescent kids made do with "necking" and "petting." Only the most daring and reckless teens "went all the way." It was a time when condoms were the only form of birth control generally available, and even they could not be legally sold for the purposes of birth control, but were required to carry the fiction "for the prevention of diseases only" on their packages. It was a time when gonorrhea and syphilis were the only venereal diseases generally available, a time when statistics on out-of-wedlock teen pregnancies weren't even kept.

It's different now. For parents *and* kids. And while it's not quite Apocalypse Now, we're getting close. There is the AIDS epidemic. There are almost half a million teen *births* annually. The number of teen *pregnancies,* about half of which are aborted, is closer to a million. According to the best evidence available—surveys, polls, estimates by researchers—50 percent of teens over fourteen are engaging in sex, a substantial proportion of that number frequently and with multiple partners and, more often than not, without the use of birth-control measures. What's a parent to do in the face of such an ominous array of statistics? "Keeping it simple" can take you just so far in an increasingly complicated and hazardous sexploitative world.

Educate Yourself — One thing you can do is educate yourself. Find out what you need to know to adequately educate your kids on such subjects as human sexuality and reproduction, failure (and success) rates of various kinds of birth-control products, the dangers of date rape, and that terrifying terminal disease with the ironically positive sounding acronym, AIDS.

Avoid scare tactics. If kids scared easily, they wouldn't be the only population segment in which smoking is on the increase. Present your material in a calm, factual, non-patronizing manner. Concentrate on a few crucially important ideas. In teaching kids about AIDS, concentrate on three basic points: 1) explain that it is transmitted through sexual contact and is invariably fatal (other transmission modes can be discussed later); 2) explain that, generally speaking, you can't get it *unless* you engage in sexual intercourse or other sexual intimacies (again, issues of *eventual* sexual intercourse, with its concomitant issues of constancy versus promiscuity, can be reserved for later); 3) explain that because of the way the AIDS virus is constructed, the likelihood that a cure, or even a vaccine, will be found in the foreseeable future is virtually zero (here again, save the complexities of the relationship between HIV and AIDS for later).

However you approach the subject of unwanted pregnancy with your kids, the birth control versus abstinence issue is bound to come up. One way to deal with this difficult dichotomy without completely begging the question is to impress on them what a remarkably effective baby-making machine the human reproductive system is—and that "unprotected" sex is the reproductive equivalent of Russian roulette with all the chambers filled. It's not an accident when you *get* pregnant; it's an accident when you *don't*.

You Are the One — An extraordinary range of individuals and institutions wants to help teach your children about sex. Notable among them are the "do it" crowd, with its "raunch, rock, and rap" version of the three R's; the "abstinence (or just say no)" crowd; and the condom crowd, led by Surgeon General Joycelyn Elders, who features a bouquet of brightly colored condoms on her desk.

While all schools of thought should be taken into account and evaluated, it is important to remember that you are your child's first teacher. When it comes to the crucial, compelling, and consequential area of sex, you are the one!

Only you are in a position to follow the biblical imprecation, "Raise up your child in the way that he [or she] should go." Only you are in a position to arm your daughter against the slings and arrows of outrageous sexual peer pressure that inevitably coincide with puberty. Only you know your daughter well enough to decide whether you can successfully make the case for abstinence—and only you can make the far more difficult judgment concerning to what extent advice about birth control will undermine that case. Only you can inoculate your son against the ugly and destructive macho code of counting sexual coups. And only you are standing at ground zero of the permanent continuous sexplosion with which your youngster must eventually cope.

But don't panic. Just hang in there and take your best shot at teaching your kids about sex without making a complete fool of yourself.

Why Is It That . . .

. . . kids jump up and down with excitement about going to a restaurant, but when they get there don't even get the seat warm?

127 Relatively Safe and Harmless Things You Can Do with Balloons: A Rainy-Day Activity for Brain-Dead Parents

It has been raining so long that God's directive to Noah has called itself up on your intercranial internet: "And God said to Noah: Make thee an ark of gopher wood and pitch it within and without with pitch." You have long since exhausted the distractive possibilities of TV, video, board games, card games, and Legos. Ditto your supply of camp songs, tales from your childhood, and repeatable jokes. Your children are confronting you with that baleful "Well, dummy, what're we going to do next?" look. The worm of panic is beginning to stir in your gizzard. Any nanosecond now, you are going to lose it and exit into the downpour and run screaming down the street.

"Look," your childless neighbor will say. "There goes X again running down the street doing his/her imitation of Munch's 'The Scream.' Better call the police. And tell them to stop off at Animal Control and pick up the big dog net."

What's it worth to you to avoid such a calamity? Is it worth laying in a supply of balloons (that's right, ordinary balloons)? A bulk supply of balloons can provide hours of relatively safe and harmless distraction. And it's a lot cheaper than building an ark. Even if you could find the gopher wood.

Is there a downside to the upside of balloon play? Isn't there always? First, you've got to blow up the damn things (balloon pumps are for sissies). And the condensation of your misty moisty breath inside the balloons makes for quite a lot of dribbling spit (but spit-valve problems never stopped Bix or Louis). Nor is there any question that extended balloon play can be messy and rowdy. So wear old clothes and hide your Hummel collection.

Here, on an ascending scale of complexity and richness, are 127 things you can do with balloons.

1. Blow 'em Up and Let 'em Fly

You will need: plenty of balloons and plenty of breath.
Object of game: to blow 'em up and let 'em fly.
Instructions: just blow 'em up and let 'em fly.

2. *Talking Balloons*

You will need: one balloon and enough breath with which to blow it up.

Object of game: to make funny noises.

Instructions: blow up balloon, then by grasping the neck with the thumbs and forefingers of both hands, inhibit deflation by stretching it taut. By alternately relaxing and tightening the neck of the balloon, it can be made to "talk."

3. *Head Boppers*

You will need: pieces of broken balloon (broken balloons are an inevitable by-product of all balloon play).

Object of game: to make loud noises by bursting balloon bubbles on the nearest noggin (advisedly your own; only children with the sturdiest of psyches will suffer being bopped without taking revenge).

Instructions: stretch a piece of broken balloon over slightly parted lips, suck in sharply, trap the resulting bubble by twisting its neck, then "bop."

4. *Balloon Aloft*

You will need: one inflated round balloon.

Object of game: to keep balloon aloft.

Instructions: the players cooperate in keeping the balloon in the air by tapping it gently. An "edge" can be introduced by keeping count of the number of taps accomplished before the balloon encounters the floor. Adults may choose to play "balloon aloft" while lying on the floor. This will allow you to take short naps while the balloon is in the air, but it also runs you the risk of getting stomped.

5. Balloon Volleyball

You will need: a "volleyball" setup. The simplest arrangement consists of a length of waxed paper or aluminum foil rigged between two high-backed chairs. Also one inflated balloon.

Object of the game: to keep the balloon aloft by tapping it back and forth over the net.

Instructions: just think of it as "slo-mo" volleyball and you'll do fine.

6. Balloon Punching Bag

You will need: a round balloon, a large rubber band cut so as to constitute a rubber string, a few dried beans or grains of rice.

Object of game: to punch the heck out of the balloon.

Instructions: introduce the beans or rice into the balloon, inflate the balloon, knot its neck, then tie one end of the "string" to the balloon, and while holding the other end punch the heck out of the balloon. You can add to the fun by allowing your kid to draw a face on the balloon and label it *Daddy*.

7. Whisper Jet

You will need: a balloon, a paper airplane, masking or two-sided tape.

Object of game: to advance aeronautical science by exploring the possibilities of jet-powered flight.

Instructions: with a bit of two-sided sticky tape or a small loop of ordinary masking tape, attach an inflated balloon to a paper airplane and let 'er fly! The possibilities inherent in the concept of balloon-powered paper airplane flight are . . .

But wait! Look, it stopped raining! And the sun's coming out! Hey, come on, kids! Let's go out and see if there's a rainbow!

What's that, you say? We promised you 127 things and that's only 7? What about the other 120 things?

Hey, it's a fair complaint if you want to be a spoilsport. But wouldn't you rather come with the rest of us and see if there's a rainbow?

Why Is It That . . .

. . . third-graders are in awe of lordly eleven-year-old sixth-graders, but have absolutely no respect for their thirty-five-year-old parents?

Short Takes III

Never Give an All-Day-Sucker an Even Break — **Recognize** that lollipops, ice cream, jams, jellies, and other sticky comestibles are magnetically attracted to stainable surfaces and strictly proscribe them from any room that is not entirely washable.

Your Child's Tabula Rasa May Be Preferable to Your Full Slate — While it's probably true that your young child doesn't know much, it's even more probably the case that you know a great many things that aren't necessarily so.

Beware the Treacherous Gonads — It's important that you grind your values axes before puberty strikes. Because once it does, you won't ever be able to get your preteen's attention. From then on it's only the residual influence of the input from those early years that you can (or can't) count on to get them through the peer-pressure years.

Don't Try to Con a Con — Children are not necessarily born liars, but they get the hang of it pretty quickly, and before long become fairly adept at distortion, shifting blame, leaving things out, and flat-out lying. Kids may not know which fork to use or which wine goes with what, but they know when they're being conned. Even very young children can pick up inconsistency, hypocrisy, and temporizing behavior on the part of their parents—and they're just the right height for attacking feet of clay.

Comes the Dawn — A school of thought among biological researchers proposes that there are sound biological reasons for your two-year-old's pronounced tendency to wake up at dawn. Their theory runs like this: It is well established that virtually all primates—gorillas, orangutans, chimpanzees, baboons, and all shapes and sizes of monkeys—wake up at dawn. Since it is equally well established that Homo sapiens is every bit as much a primate as those guys who stare back at us so accusingly at the zoo, it's perfectly natural for your two-year-old to wake up at dawn. It's your own tendency to "sleep in" as long as you possibly can that's unnatural. A nonscientific, nonresearch group (parents) strongly opposes this we're-all-monkeys-under-the-skin theory of reveille. This group holds that two-year-olds wake up at dawn to express their resentment at our having brought them into the world without their having been asked.

"Mommy, What're Rape, Gay Rights, and Abortion?": How to Deal with Those Difficult Questions You'd Rather Never Came Up

It follows as surely as the morning follows the night before that as our society binges on ever greater openness and freedom of information, parents are going to have to deal with questions that older generations of parents never even asked, much less had to answer.

Here are some thoughts and ideas that may help you prepare yourself for the interrogation.

1. *Anticipate Likely Questions and Think About How Best to Answer Them* — Since stammering, stuttering, and rolling your eyes are at the very least undignified, it would be well to anticipate some of the more obvious questions so that you can deal with them with at least a modicum of dignity and coherence.

2. *Face the Fact that TV Has Eliminated the Age of Innocence* — With panel discussions about impotence, the G spot, and transvestite rights, and newsbreaks about rape and mass murder just a channel hop away from Big Bird and Mr. Rogers, it is all but inevitable that you are going to be called upon to answer some very challenging questions. You can, to a certain extent, postpone the inevitable by rigorously limiting your child's viewing to suitable programming. Channel hopping can be eliminated by the simple (but expensive) expedient of procuring one of the new knobless sets and retaining strict control of the remote control.

3. *Answer Difficult Questions as Promptly and Straight-forwardly as Possible, but Avoid Dissertations* — It is usually possible to frame an appropriate answer on any subject on which a child has managed to frame a question. Keep your answer simple and brief. Sample question and answer: "Mommy, what're test-tube babies?" "Well, sweetie, you know how usually babies grow inside the mommy's belly"— we *presume* you've already gotten *that* out of the way—"well, some mommies can't get babies started, so scientists and doctors have figured out a way to get the baby started outside the mommy's belly, then put it in afterward."

If the issue in question is a highly controversial one, it may be useful to suggest that different people have different ideas on the subject. If your child wants to know what you think, by all means state your case.

4. *The "Rain Check" Option* — Sometimes, because of the press of other business or a potentially awkward situation involving others, it is necessary, even advisable, to postpone the answer to an important question. This is acceptable to most children, provided you have a good track record of honoring rain checks. As with really tough questions, a brief postponement offers the advantage of giving you a chance to figure out just what the heck you're going to say.

5. *Try to Moderate Your Answers in Areas Where You Hold Immoderate Opinions* — A young child is really not equipped to deal with the emotional head of steam a parent may have built up over the years. Which is to say, just because you are a nut on a particular subject—dogs running loose, Richard Nixon, or zoysia grass—is no reason to saddle your child with your preoccupations.

6. *If You Don't Know the Answer to a Question, Admit It Freely* — Nowhere is it written that your role as Junior's first teacher requires you to be omniscient. Usually it will come as something of a relief to your child to have you admit what was long suspected: that you don't know all the answers. Indeed, one of the greatest gifts you can bestow upon a child is the knowledge that there is a prodigious lot left in the world to find out and that he or she might just be the one to fill in a couple of the blanks.

Whad'jabringme? and Other Games Children Play

Whad'jabringme?

Played as follows: Junior stands about ten feet from the front door. When he hears Daddy, who has been out of town for a few days, approaching, he assumes the attack crouch position (leaning slightly forward on the balls of the feet ready to spring). When Daddy appears in the doorway, Junior becomes a human cannonball without benefit of cannon and crashes into Daddy about chest high. The game ends with Daddy carrying Junior over to the sofa, where he takes an airport tchotchkila from his briefcase and bestows it on Junior.

A variant of whad'jabringme? involves an altered endgame. This version is appropriate for those occasions when both Daddy *and* Mommy go out of town for a few days and leave Junior with a sitter. This version plays out as follows: Instead of screaming "Whad'jabringme?" and leaping at his parents, Junior just sits there playing with his Playmobil castle set. He doesn't even look up. It's Daddy and Mommy who have the lines in this version. "Sweetheart! We're home!" they cry. "And guess what we brought you!" Junior looks at the proffered package. He hefts it for weight. He puts it aside. He'll open it later—and it better be more than some damn airport tchotchkila.

I Don't Hafta.

Played as follows: As you pull into the last-chance-to-fill-up-for-two-hundred-miles gas station, you gently raise the issue of "emptying out" with your youngster. "I don't hafta," repostes your youngster. You revisit the issue a number of times during your stay at the gas station and a number of times are told, "I don't hafta." The game ends about sixty-seven miles into the Mojave Desert when your youngster turns to you and says, "I hafta."

Hide-and-Peek.

Played in exactly the same manner as hide-and-seek, with the following exception: The youngest player is allowed to cheat.

Jump on Daddy.

A game in which Daddy lies on the floor and suffers his child to jump, roll, and climb on him at will. While this game is relatively unstructured, there are some rules: The child may not weigh more than thirty-five pounds and must remove his or her shoes. Neither is the child permitted to sit on Daddy's face or jump from an elevated point like the sofa or coffee table.

Hide-and-Poop.

This game comes into play in the farther and more difficult reaches of toilet training when the child is clinging to diapers and the parents are clinging to the fantasy that little Jack or Jill will someday be using the potty. The game is simplicity itself: The child finds some secret, hard-to-find loading zone, while the parents try to figure out where the hell he or she is. (They *know* what he or she is doing.)

Spin Till You Drop.

Played as follows: The parent watches as the child spins around and around until he or she gets dizzy and drops. This is repeated until the parent becomes concerned lest the child get hurt. Ignoring the parent's expressions of concern, the child does one more spin, falls heavily against the étagère, incurs a minor forehead cut, and cries for two or three hours.

Counsel from the Codger

When a codgerish old friend of ours asked what we were doing lately, we answered that we were still "doing our thing," creating books about a bear family who "live down a sunny dirt road deep in Bear Country," but that we were also working on a book for grown-ups called *What Your Parents Never Told You About Being a Mom or Dad.*

After a noncommittal "Hmm," followed by a long pause, he launched into a jeremiad on the inadvisability of having, raising, and especially being a child today. "It's all high-tech, battery-operated, computerized, digitalized video junk! It may be kids watching screens today, but if we don't watch out, tomorrow it'll be screens watching screens! What ever happened to simplicity? What ever happened to skipping stones on a pond, fishing with a bent pin, telling time by dandelion, blowing on an empty Good & Plenty box and making a whistling sound during the kissing scenes at the movies, stamping on empty quart oil cans so they'd bend onto your shoe soles and make a helluva racket when you stomped around on them?"

The codger is not a man to argue with or interrupt, so we just listened until he ran out of steam. Then we thanked him for his point of view and asked if he had any suggestions for our book—perhaps some low-tech ideas that might recapture the spirit of simplicity he was talking about. "Got some doozies," he replied. "And all I'm gonna need is a brown paper bag, a clean white hanky, and my own two hands." He then proceeded to explicate and demonstrate the Invisible Coin Trick, Babies in the Cradle, and the Church and the Steeple. We pass them along for your consideration.

1. The Invisible Coin Trick

You will need:
one paper bag.
How to do trick:
Hold the bag as
shown. Hold up the
"invisible coin."
Then say, "Now I
shall toss this
invisible coin up and
catch it in the bag."

Pretend to toss
the coin in the air,
and move the bag to "catch" it. At that moment, *snap the
fingers of the hand holding the bag.* The bag will shake and

SNAP!

make a noise as if
you were catching
a real coin.

Next, reach into
the bag and pretend
to remove the coin.
Hold it up and ask if
anyone would like to
see the trick again.

2. Babies in the Cradle

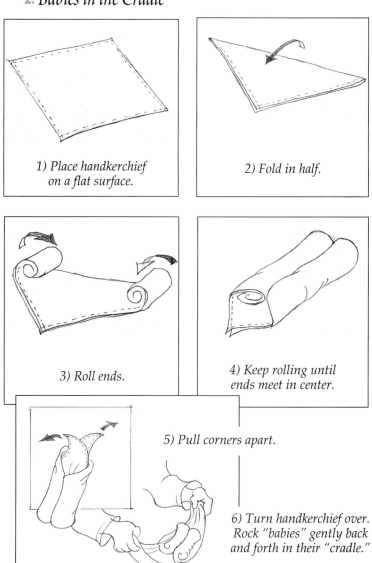

1) Place handkerchief on a flat surface.

2) Fold in half.

3) Roll ends.

4) Keep rolling until ends meet in center.

5) Pull corners apart.

6) Turn handkerchief over. Rock "babies" gently back and forth in their "cradle."

3. The Church and the Steeple

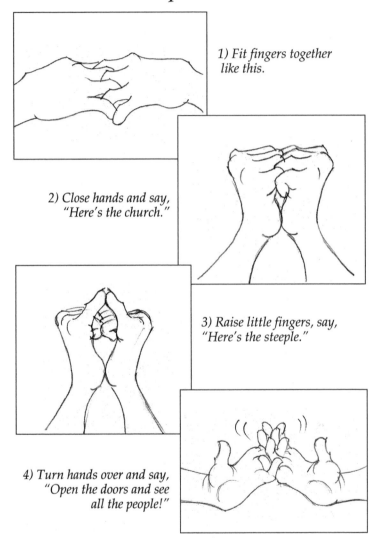

1) Fit fingers together like this.

2) Close hands and say, "Here's the church."

3) Raise little fingers, say, "Here's the steeple."

4) Turn hands over and say, "Open the doors and see all the people!"

Apocalypse Now?

After graduating college some years ago, a young man we know joined VISTA and participated in the founding of a day-care center in northern Wisconsin. He then went on to teach at the center, which was located in the basement of a Lutheran church.

It was a lively sort of place which offered its two- to five-year-old denizens a program of activities and early education. It featured snack time, nap time, run-amuck time, and story time. One of the early ed offerings was a daily lesson on the calendar. Each month a large calendar would be drawn up, and at the end of each day the teacher would talk to the kids about such arcane notions as the day of the week, the month of the year, and how they both followed one upon the other.

"As I've been telling you," he said, "the name of this month is November. And this," he continued, pointing to the appropriate box, "is the day where we are now. The next box shows tomorrow, and the next box shows the day after tomorrow. And after that there won't be any more days in November. Okay, now let's all say No-*vem*-ber."

"No-*vem*-ber!" said all assembled.

By now moms and dads had arrived to pick up their kids. The teacher was performing his usual end-of-session duties, greeting parents, helping kids on with their coats, explaining to some kids that their parents would be a few minutes late, when he noticed that four-year-old Caitlin, normally a cheerful child, was crying.

The teacher knelt beside her. "Caitlin," he said. "Whatever is the matter?"

Caitlin pointed to the calendar and, through her tears,

sobbed, "Y-y-you said there weren't going to be any more days!"

It took a while to console the little girl and to convince her that the calendar lesson had to do with the end of *November* and *not* the end of the world.

The experience taught both the teacher and the child valuable lessons. It taught the teacher that you have to be very careful about what you say to little children. It taught the child not to put too much stock in what grown-ups tell you.

The Day-Care Quandary—A Checklist

Some things about the experience of parenthood haven't changed very much—the miracle of tiny fingers and toes hasn't changed at all; the fretful bane of colic and the angst of teething have been preserved intact.

But some things do change—rapidly and radically. In the past twenty years the number of working mothers in the population has grown from 17 percent to over 50 percent. This enormous change raises many issues, not the least of which is the matter of child care. What years ago was generally a judgment call—will nursery school (day care, as such, was largely unavailable as late as the fifties and early sixties) be good for little Jill or Johnny? is he or she too young? is there a shortage of kids in the neighborhood? etc.—has become as urgent a necessity as food and shelter.

Indeed, finding adequate child care so you can keep on working has a considerable bearing on whether you will be able to *afford* food and shelter in this perpetually difficult economy.

Since you need all the help you can get—the pressures of parenthood also being perpetual—here is a checklist of some of the factors to be considered when choosing a day-care facility. As with so many of the problems and concerns of parenthood, common sense is much more important than special knowledge.

1. *Select the Best Facility You Can Afford, but Be Realistic*—Avoid the trap of wishful thinking and be realistic about your ability to afford the glossiest facility in town. This is going to be a long-term expense. Remember: Overbuying in this area can bust your budget just as drastically as the monthly payments on the Volvo you want but can't afford.

2. *Child Care Is Primarily a "People Business"*—It has been said that every business is a people business. In no area is this more to the point than in the matter of choosing a day-care facility. The quality and quantity of personnel is much more important than the latest word in plant and equipment. It's people that care for children—not stainless steel minikitchens and mint collections of Fisher-Price preschool toys.

3. *Visit the Facility While It's in Session*—If management would prefer a cozy chat in the administrator's office after the evidence has all gone home, regard the establishment with suspicion.

Observe the nature of the interaction between the kids and the care-giving staff. Do the kids generally appear to like the "teachers"? Is there plenty of unforced cuddling and comforting of the kids who seem to want it and need it, and a respectful "hands off" policy for kids who prefer to interact in other ways—like beating the teacher at chess, for example?

4. *Seek Firsthand-Experience Recommendations from Parents You Know and Trust* —When seeking good child care—or a good gynecologist, acupuncturist, or divorce lawyer, for that matter—there is no substitute for the recommendations of fellow sufferers who have been there.

5. *Does the Space and Operational Format of the Facility Allow for a Flexible, Interactive Schedule?* —Day care works best when children are permitted to move in and out of various types of activities as their individual needs and attention spans require—perhaps quiet puzzle play for a while, then maybe a quick dip into the maelstrom of action play, then perhaps a little role playing in the doll corner.

Of course, there is a need for an overall schedule involving such events as opening class, mealtime, nap time, snack time, story hour, and so on, but it is the substructure created by the child him- or herself that gives the child that sense of autonomy that even the youngest toddler needs.

6. *The Mayhem Factor* — During your visit to a prospective day-care center, make a rough count of cuts, bruises, black eyes, and broken limbs in the school population. If the count is impressive, ask questions. If answers are not forthcoming, be forewarned. Not that a school population that looks like the Wild Bunch is *necessarily* disqualifying. If your youngster is the type that's more likely to give than to receive, you may figure *c'est la guerre* and sign him up.

Why Is It That . . .

. . . T-ball sluggers who regularly hit doubles and triples can't figure out you're supposed to run to second base?

On the Persistence of Belief in Santa Claus, the Easter Bunny, the Wishing Star, and the Tooth Fairy

Young parents simply can't wait to introduce their toddlers to the joys and vicissitudes of Santa Claus and his seasonally activated egg-hiding, wish-granting, coin-leaving colleagues. Neophyte parents become positively giddy as they anticipate the magical moments attendant on these encounters: the look in their little darling's eyes on Christmas morning, the headlong excitement of the Easter egg hunt, the sweet innocence of that first wish upon a star, that triumphant shout of "The Tooth Fairy came!" as gap-toothed Junior runs into Mommy and Daddy's bedroom, coin held high.

But when Junior gets to be four and five, the charm of leaving milk and cookies for Santa and carrot sticks for the Easter Bunny, dealing with the first star and the fourteenth deciduous tooth, begins to wear off, and exhaustion sets in. What about *that*? Mom and Dad begin to wonder if Junior's got good sense. After all, the kid's got to start growing up, thinking things through, applying logic. How the heck is he going to get into MIT or Virginia Polytechnic Institute if he still believes in Santa Claus, the Easter Bunny, the Wishing Star, and the Tooth Fairy!

Mom and Dad begin to grouse. How can any kid of theirs be so dumb as not to be able to figure out that Santa couldn't *possibly* deliver all those toys to all the kids in the world in just one night? And since when can reindeer fly? As for Junior's persistent belief in Santa's colleagues, the chocoholic bunny, the zillion-miles-away Wishing Star, and that morbid bicuspid collector, the Tooth Fairy—forget about them! Grow up! Get a paper route!

But we ask you, Mom and Dad, are you being entirely fair, dumping on beliefs you so assiduously pounded into Junior's tender consciousness? What about all those other unexamined beliefs floating around out there? What about all the unexamined beliefs of cultures and civilizations of ages gone by? What about your own unexamined beliefs: the idea that everything will work out, that tomorrow will be a better day, that a copper bracelet will mitigate the discomforts of arthritis, that the respective positions of the stars and planets on the day you were born just might have some bearing on whether today is a good day for investments—any number of beliefs no more or less supportable than Junior's quartet of faith assumptions?

Between you and your kid, Junior's got the better deal. After all, he's getting *beaucoup* toys, chocolate eggs, fulfilled wishes, and coins of the realm (though we hear the price of a tooth has escalated to at least a dollar).

Hey, bubbies, what are you getting out of your dopey beliefs?

Varieties of Religious Experience

The first grade library of Winslow School was so small (it was really a converted supply closet) it accommodated only two children at a time. First graders Steve and Danny were sitting on the bench that served as a staging area for the library. They would remain there until Fay and Elma emerged with their chosen books. Then Steve and Danny would take their turn in the library and two more children would come out of class to wait on the bench. Fay and Elma were taking rather long, which gave Steve, who came from a religious tradition which held that the miraculous events of the Bible were literally true, a chance to tell Danny about *The Ten Commandments,* a movie he had just seen over the weekend. Danny, on the other hand, came from a tradition that saw the Bible as a wise and holy book, but one that was subject to interpretation.

"You shoulda seen it," said Steve, his eyes alight. "The 'Gyptians were chasing the Isreals and they came to the Red Sea and the 'Gyptians were gonna get 'em and make 'em into slaves again. But then Moses prayed to God for help, and you shoulda seen it! The Red Sea opened up! It just opened up and the Isreals went through it just like it was dry land! But when the 'Gyptians started after 'em, the whole sea—it was like a ocean—closed in and they all got drownded and the Isreals got away! I mean, you shoulda seen it! It was a miracle!"

"Well," said Danny, with some discomfort. "It sounds like a really good movie and I'm probly gonna see it. But I have to tell you, Steve, I've got my own ideas about miracles."

"Whadaya mean?" said Steve. "I tell you, I saw it with my own eyes! And seein' is believin'!"

"Okay, you two," said the teacher. "You can go into the library now. Fay and Elma are finished."

It was Danny's three-and-a-half-year-old little brother, Zack, that Mom and Dad were concerned about in connection with their planned trip to see *The Ten Commandments.* There was no way they were going to get away with leaving him home with a sitter. But they were concerned that all the violence and strangeness he would see on the screen would confuse and upset him. They explained that they were going to see a grown-up movie about the Bible and if there was anything he wondered about—anything at all—he should ask questions.

There was an air of expectancy in the theater as the house lights dimmed. The opening strains of the musical score filled the theater as the main titles were emblazoned on the screen in magnificent red and gold. As befitted as colossal a production as Cecil B. De Mille's *The Ten Commandments,* the opening titles were rather lengthy. When they got to the fine print identifying the second unit's third assistant grip, Zack tapped his father on the knee.

"Yes, son, do you have a question?"

"Yeah," said Zack. "When's it gonna start?"

A couple of houses up the street from Danny and Zack, five-year-old Vickie's mom and dad were having an awful row about her starting Sunday school. Vickie's mom was absolutely bound and determined that Vickie should attend Sunday school. Her daddy didn't care whether she did or not.

You never heard such screaming and hollering.

Little Tommy was kneeling by his bed and saying his prayers. "Now I lay me down to sleep/ I pray the Lord my soul to keep/ If I should die before I wake/ I pray the lord my soul to take." After a "Bless Mommy," a "Bless Daddy," and a couple of kisses good night, he climbed under the covers and was soon fast asleep.

During the night a terrible storm arose. Thunder shook the earth. Jagged streaks of lightning lacerated the sky. Little

Tommy woke up in a state of terror. He leaped out of bed and ran to his parents' room screaming, "He's trying to get me! He's trying to get me!" And he leaped into bed with Mom and Dad.

"Who's trying to get you, sweetie?" asked Mom.

Tommy stated his belief, based on the evidence of the storm, that God was trying to get him.

"Oh no, sweetie. God loves you," said his mother. "God loves you very much."

"Yeah," said Tommy, as another lightning strike split the sky. "Then how come he's trying to get me?"

The centerpiece of Grandparents' Day at Friends Country Day School was worship in the historic Quaker meetinghouse that stood on the campus. The school's headmaster opened the meeting by explaining to those present who were not Quakers that Quakers did not have clergy and worshiped by ministering to each other. "We sit quietly," he went on to explain, "and speak when the spirit moves us." After what seemed a rather long silence, broken only by the coughs of wheezy grandparents, the spirit moved a woman to rise and say, "I have just come from the wedding of my forty-two-year-old daughter, who was just married for the first time. Praise the Lord!"

Under the cover of the tittering that followed, eight-year-old Charlene turned to her grandfather and whispered, "Was she trying to be funny?" "Well," said her grandfather, beginning to formulate an answer. But the tittering had died and Charlene shushed her grandfather vociferously.

Though five-year-old Gwen's dad had done a pretty good job of making the case for God as master of the universe and creator of all things, Gwen was a thoughtful child, and one day when she and her dad were walking to a small nearby park, she decided to test the concept.

"Daddy," she said.

"Yes, Gwennie."

"You know how you said God made the whole world?"

"Yes," said Dad. "And everything in it."

"And the solar system with all the planets and the sun and all?"

"Everything in the *universe,* Gwennie," said Dad, congratulating himself for having helped his daughter make a model of the solar system out of wire and different kinds of fruit. Of course, the grapes hadn't worked out. And it was hell drilling those walnuts.

"And the dry holes and the seven dwarfs?"

"Black holes and dwarf stars, sweetie." Perhaps he *should* have stopped with the solar system, as his wife had suggested. "That's right, dear. The whole universe and everything in it."

As they entered the park, they passed a box elder tree that was clotted with accumulations of tent caterpillars.

"How about tent caterpillars?" asked Gwen. "Did God make tent caterpillars?"

Daddy sighed. "I'm not sure *why* He made tent caterpillars, Gwennie, but the answer is yes, God made tent caterpillars."

"And birds and flowers and worms and dogs and cats?"

"That's right, sweetie," said Dad, trying to put a lid on it. "God made the whole entire universe and everything in it. Now, what do you say we try to forget about God for a while and enjoy our walk. It's such a beautiful day. Hey, I know what. Let's climb the hill to the gazebo. You can see the whole town from up there."

"Daddy."

"Yes."

"Remember when Clara got in heat and got out one night and got run over by a truck?"

"I remember."

"Did God make Clara get in heat and get out the window and get run over by a truck?"

"Look," said Daddy. "You're a wonderful little girl and you ask some very good questions, and I'm going to do my best to answer them. Yes, God made cats. So I guess you could say God made cats get in heat . . . but as far as Clara getting out and . . . well, it's not that simple."

Gwen and her dad had ascended the hill and were standing in the gazebo. They were looking out over the entire town. They could see the houses and trees, the school, the box factory, the cemetery where Dad's parents were buried, the failed downtown business district, the mall just outside of town. They looked out in silence for a long time.

"Dad," said Gwen.

"Yes, Gwennie."

"What about questions?"

"I don't get you, Gwennie."

"Well, what I want to know is, did God make questions?"

"Yes," said Dad after a considerable pause. "I think it's fair to say that God made questions—*mostly* questions."

How to Undermine Junior's Teacher

*A Compendium of
Complaints from Ms. Arbani,
Ms. Guilfoyle, and Mr. Marple*

It's no secret that our schools are under stress and that teachers have problems. Many if not most teachers are handicapped by outsize classes, inadequate supplies of textbooks and materials, and outdated material. But we tend to overlook the peskiest problem: ourselves!

The fact is that many of us parents work so hard at undermining Junior's teacher that it's a wonder she (or he) can do the job at all. Some acts of teacher sabotage are committed even before Junior ventures inside the school.

"Oh, you'll just *love* kindergarten," says Mother to little Baxter, tears of joy welling from her eyes as she thinks of that big yellow bus coming to take little Baxter away. "All you do is play and play and play!" (The *plans* Mommy has for herself!) "And there's this wonderful, pretty lady with a sweet voice who reads you wonderful stories." (Shopping trips, fashion shows, card parties!) "Oh, Baxter, it'll be simply heavenly!"

The big day comes and off floats Baxter fully expecting kindergarten to be a magical dreamland presided over by the Blue Fairy. When it turns out to be nothing more than a big room with stuff all put away in closets and chairs to sit on and a big rug to rest on and milk to drink (*white* milk, at that!) and a lady who keeps telling you to sit down, he's fit to be tied. Ms. Arbani considers doing just that, but decides to exhaust conventional disciplinary methods first.

Once the term gets under way, the agony of kindergarten

begins in earnest. Julia shows up with a damp little sticky creature she claims is her brother. "My mommy says can he be in kindergarten today 'cause she has to go somewheres!"

Howard checks in four Mondays in a row without milk money. "Mommy dint have no change, just a thirty-dollar bill." The class as a whole is into the teacher for a cool $16.45.

A little bottle marked JANIE'S NOSE DROPS—2 DROPS IN EACH NOSTRIL EVERY HOUR turns up on the teacher's desk.

Then there's that unspeakable crew (probably the same ones who keep voting down those school bond issues) who send kids to kindergarten in clothes that they can't manage— such unmanipulables as cloverleaf-zippered snowpants, coats with $\frac{3}{4}$-inch buttons and $\frac{1}{2}$-inch buttonholes, boots with bent snaps, and a pair of too-small underpants . . . on backwards. Is it any wonder there's a desperate Blue Fairy shortage?

Ms. Arbani's principal beef is that some parents can't get it through their heads that kindergarten is an important part of the educational program, not a glorified sitting service. Kindergarten teaching is one of the most demanding jobs in the whole field of education. The brave souls who take it on deserve better of us than damp sticky little brothers and escape-proof underwear. (If you want to get a rough idea what it's like, throw a party for your child's kindergarten class.)

The first grade teacher's main complaint about parents is that they tend to "choke up" when it finally dawns on them that next term Junior will be in *first grade!* Little Junior, who just yesterday was crawling around the floor eating dust devils, will have to learn to read and write and do sums!

Mothers, particularly, are subject to first-grade choke up. It may take hold as early as the last day of kindergarten when Junior brings home that fateful little card, the one that says,

"At the opening of school on Thursday, September 10, Junior Jones will be placed in grade 1, room 7. His teacher will be Ms. Guilfoyle."

"Ms. Guilfoyle, huh?" Mother tries to think which one is Ms. Guilfoyle. Is it the tall slim one or the little blonde with bangs? Or maybe it's that good-looking young redhead with the figure. What can *she* know about what it means to raise a child, to nourish him, to walk the floor nights, to bring him through measles and chicken pox and cut knees and? . . . A terrible thought occurs to Mother. Suppose this Ms. Guilfoyle person doesn't *like* him, just takes an irrational dislike to him, then decides he's *stupid*. Then a *really* terrible thought occurs to her. Suppose it turns out that Junior *is* stupid, or has a "reading block," or is a "mirror writer," or isn't ready for "number concepts"!

First-grade choke up can be a fearsome thing. Almost overnight it can turn a perfectly reasonable woman into a skulking rumormonger. "Ms. Guilfoyle? Oh, yes, I know about her. She's a terror, screams at them from the time they get in to the time they leave." "Isn't she the local rep of the NEA? Sends everybody to the school psychologist." "Ms. Guilfoyle—isn't she the one who . . . ?" "Oh, yes, Ms. Guilfoyle's the gal that . . ." And so on until the dossier is complete.

The tragic thing is that almost inevitably such gossip is communicated to Junior, and, though it's seldom fatal, it can lead to serious complications. Things like reading block, mirror writing, and number trouble.

As if things aren't sour enough, who should blunder onto the scene but Daddy. He has somehow sensed that something important is about to happen and, calling on his animal cunning, has somehow figured out that Junior is going into first grade.

"What happened to kindergarten? Don't they go to kindergarten first?" he asks, sniffing the air with his trunk, his great ragged ears rippling in the light breeze.

"He *went* to kindergarten."

"With all the finger paint and blocks and everything?"

"Yep."

"Hmmm."

The great beast is perturbed.

The training of the young is a serious matter. Has he allowed the female to take too much upon herself? Perhaps it's not too late. With a shake of his great head, he lumbers over to where Junior is grazing at the edge of the herd, and addresses him. Son"— advice to young ele- phants: When they start calling you Son, lookout —"Son, I understand you're about to enter first grade. You realize, of course, the impor- tance of first grade. Everything you do in school from now on goes into your permanent record. You've got a good mind and a good background, so there's no reason why you shouldn't be at the top of your class. Do I make myself clear? NOW, YOU

GO RIGHT INTO THAT FIRST GRADE AND *DO A JOB!"* he bellows, and crashes off through the underbrush.

And what does Junior do? He goes right into the first grade and does a job. He throws up all over the place.

With the children finally in school, Ms. Guilfoyle can start getting them ready for the first-grade program. (Incidentally, she turns out to be the one with the figure, so at least there won't be any difficulty getting Daddy to PTA meetings.) She knows from experience that she can expect to have about three weeks comparatively free of parental sabotage. It takes that long for parents to realize that their kids are actually in first grade and that nothing really terrible is going to happen to them. Then, too, parents are kept pretty busy those first weeks—worrying about the school bus situation, for example.

"Junior, why do you keep getting on the *wrong bus?* Don't you recognize your driver?"

"Sure. He has a red face, a big black mustache, big eyebrows, a gold tooth, and he's real grouchy."

"Then why don't you get on his bus?"

"I'm scared."

By the end of three weeks, however, parents are ready to get back into the act. "What's going on at the school?" they ask. "All he's brought home is a paper of crooked *1*s, and some forms for us to fill out."

When one of the forms turns out to be an invitation to the year's first PTA meeting, everybody's pleased—except maybe the teacher. The purpose of this meeting is to give the teacher a chance to go over the year's program, and in this way answer any questions the parents might have. The rub is that these sessions sometimes give rise to more questions than they can answer.

In addressing the fourteen mommies and six daddies who have jammed themselves into the tiny desks, Ms. Guilfoyle makes one thing very clear. "I'd like to say right off that I'm *not* going to discuss individual children tonight." Disappointed groan from parents. "I'll be happy to talk about your children later on when there's more to talk about, but that's not our purpose tonight. Since reading is the most important part of first grade, I'm going to discuss our reading program."

Her talk is a little gem of exposition. She's very careful to explain how different children are "ready" to read at different times. She makes it very clear that the fact that Child A is ready for a certain reader today and Child B is not has *nothing* to do with intelligence. Ms. Guilfoyle tells her parents quite candidly that parents probably shouldn't be let in on all this, but that since children might be bringing home different readers and workbooks, it's much better to give a full explanation.

"What we've done is divide the class into three groups—the faster group, the middle group, and the slower group. This has nothing to do with how smart a child is. May I *stress* that fact. It has to do only with how ready he is to read, how ready his eye muscles are to do the job of scanning, how well he understands right and left, and a whole complex of factors. A child may be in the late reading group and be a brilliant child, or a child may be a perfectly astonishing reader but not so accomplished in everything else. One more important point—don't make a big thing of this with your children. It's all done very carefully. There is absolutely no stigma attached to being in the late reading group, and there's absolutely no honor attached to being in the early reading group. And remember, *it has nothing to do with intelligence.* Now, are there any questions?"

Seven hands shoot up.

"Yes? The gentleman in the checked jacket."

"I'm Joe's father. Which group is my kid in, the smart group, the ordinary group, or the dumb group?"

During the discussion that follows, Ms. Guilfoyle spots a number of other likely saboteurs. Julia's mother once read a book and is an expert on the methods of teaching reading. Jonathan's father, an IQ fancier, is disappointed to hear that the first IQ test isn't given until second grade and protests vociferously when he learns that it's the policy of the school never to give out the results anyhow. Freddy's mother wants to know if it's all right if she takes Freddy to Florida for a few weeks starting next Tuesday. Harvey's mother wants to know whether or not they serve chocolate milk in the lunchroom. Gloria's mother has a bright idea—she'll send a few dollars to school every Monday and then Ms. Guilfoyle can give Gloria lunch money each day and it'll be so much simpler that way.

Ms. Guilfoyle has one consolation: She's not alone. Similar discussions are taking place throughout the school. The higher the grade, the more insistent becomes the IQ question. Impassioned pleas for parents not to make their children overconscious of these special tests, which, after all, are intended merely as guides for educators, fall on deafer and deafer ears.

Mr. Marple, the second grade teacher, usually has to put up with a few ill-considered attacks on the first grade teacher. The third grade teacher will hear some pretty candid opinions of the second grade teacher, and so on up through the grades. These complaints about Junior's previous teacher often reflect an attitude that is deeply rankling to educators—the notion that teacher qualification rises with grade level; that is, that the second grade teacher is smarter than the first grade teacher, the third grade teacher is smarter than the second grade teacher, and so on. The idea is as pernicious as it is wrongheaded. In each grade the teacher has an important and difficult job to do. It's just as hard to teach first graders to read as it is to teach twelfth graders to balance complex chemical equations. But Junior needs to hear just once something like "Ms. Brown says he's not up to grade level, but if she's so smart, how come she's only teaching first grade?" before Ms. Brown's efforts to get *him* up to grade level are undermined.

The various PTA mucky-mucks will circulate through the school, blithely interrupting teachers with recruiting pitches for this year's Gala Big Top fund-raising affair. "We're going to need a lot of volunteers this year. We need booth tenders, ticket sellers, counter people, poster artists, publicity people. We can use carpenters, barkers, painters, and we're renting a special outfit to fill balloons with gas and we need a mechanically inclined mommy or daddy to operate it. So if you'll all fill out these little talent sheets . . ."

Last year's Gala Big Top was such a great success that the PTA was able to buy the school two more TV sets. And the mothers did it themselves. All the teachers had to do was keep teaching throughout the weeks of frenzied ticket selling, drum beating, and booth building it took to set the thing up. This year they're trying for a computer.

Most teachers realize that bringing up kids is pretty debilitating work and are willing to forgive us most of our trespasses against them. There's one parental practice, though, that teachers find pretty hard to take. It's the tendency of some parents to accept as the whole, unadulterated, unvarnished truth such

unlikely children's claims as "Whenever somebody does something, the teacher blames me" or "She purposely announced the test while I was out of the room so I'd flunk" or "She's always picking on me, like when we're having a spelling bee she gives me all the hard words."

The trouble with us parents, to state the problem in its simplest form, is that we're human. Junior's teacher, being human herself, is among the first to sympathize with our condition. She doesn't expect us to be paragons of objectivity where Junior is concerned. All she asks is that we keep our sabotage to a minimum, that we avoid cloverleaf zippers, that we give her a fighting chance to prove she's not a monster, that we keep our sense of proportion about things like reading groups and IQ test results, that we be a little more wary of educational medicine men, and that we occasionally take a look at the official objectives of the National Congress of Parents and Teachers.

Considering what Junior's teacher accomplishes while we're hacking the ground out from under her, it's interesting to contemplate what might happen if we were to stop hacking and start helping. There's no telling *what* might develop. Why, it might even turn out that Junior's a pretty darn bright youngster after all.

One in the Aisle

Of all amateur theatricals, none is more spectacularly and breathtakingly amateur than those offered by the lower cycle (first, second, and third grade) of any elementary school you care to name. The dramaturgy is the antithesis of turgid, the teacher/prompter's hisses from the wings are the "sibilants heard 'round the auditorium," the clams produced by the school orchestra are sufficiently tainted as to spread auditory hepatitis.

Your own involvement with this sort of presentation begins innocently enough a couple of weeks before Christmas when your first grader says through after-school milk and cookies, "Our school is going to put on a show and our class is gonna say a pome. Here's my part." He hands you a crumpled paper, which, when uncrumpled, reveals itself to be a computer-generated copy of Clement Moore's "A Visit from Saint Nick." Six circled lines having to do with such matters as ashes, soot, and the stump of a pipe are apparently Junior's "part." He explains with some urgency that he has to learn it by next Friday, which gives him less than two weeks, about two days a line. So, laying a finger aside of your nose, you go to work preparing Junior for his theatrical debut. Though he is normally a highly vocal, even boisterous child, his first attempt to deliver the lines comes across like he's trying out for the role of Mumbles in a presentation of "Dick Tracy." But with Daddy standing out on the back stoop in the cold shouting, "I CAN'T *HEAR* YOU!" and Mommy in the front room with Junior urging, "Louder!" his delivery improves to the point where he will at least be heard on the stage if not in the last row.

During the run-up to the show, you try to find out about the rest of the show. But extracting information about what's happening at school from your hard-to-pin-down first grader is akin to trying to fix on a mote in your aqueous humor while rolling your eyes. But something tells you you'll be rolling your eyes and worse if you attend the lowercycle show without some sense of what you're getting into.

Junior is not entirely nonforthcoming. He informs you that "some of the first and second grade girls are gonna do a graceful dance." Also, "The orchestra is gonna play some songs. There's gonna be a wooden soldier march and some other stuff. Now, can't I go out and play?"

Fair enough.

It is *der tag*. Your spouse team arrives early enough to get good seats. Good seats at lower-cycle shows are aisle seats. Though the principal evaluative criterion is ease of egress in case of an emergency (let's not speculate, at this point, what sort of emergency), aisle seats offer other advantages as well: good sight lines to the stage and good sight lines *from* the stage. Just as you want to see your kid, your kid will need to confirm that you have shown up as promised.

The audience has seated itself with a minimum of confusion and waving at friends. The orchestra, under the direction of Mr. Hoffmeister, has taken its place. A few thespians are prematurely trying to make eye contact with their parents by sneaking peeks from under and between the curtains. A teacher stands before the curtains and makes the mandatory preperformance announcements. She thanks the audience for coming. She thanks the principal, the office staff, the custodial staff, a whole raft of teachers who have worked long and hard, and, last but not least, Mr. Hoffmeister, who has prepared our magnificent school orchestra for this presentation and who will now conduct the overture.

A hush descends over the auditorium. Mr. Hoffmeister delivers a downbeat and *Wham!* a cataclysm of sound bursts over the audience like a bomb—the sort of bomb SWAT teams toss into nests of terrorists to render them helpless. It sounds like a mob of rented musical instruments gone mad, plunging ahead in full-throated pursuit of a runaway melody. But what is the melody? The program is no help. It just says "Overture." As you sit there, you begin to experience the first pangs of an awful giddiness you haven't felt since Cousin Julia's wedding, when the bride, gorgeous in an ankle-length bridal gown, lost her half-slip during the ceremony. But, mercifully, the orchestral volume is beginning to diminish. Perhaps the piece is marked *diminuendo.* Perhaps the musicians are running out of wind. But, no, they're making musical space for a solo—a *horn* solo! You breathe a prayer to Apollo, god of the lyre, to protect you from the solo. And it might have worked, except for one thing: Bracing for the solo, the horn player shifts, causing the horn to glint before emitting the biggest clam since the giant mollusk that almost put an end to John Wayne's deep-sea-diving career in the movie they show frequently on American Movie Classics.

You may have been able to handle the clam without the glint. But that premonitory glint has sealed your demise. What were mere pangs of giddiness are now powerful waves, equivalent to the waves of nausea that had folks hanging over rails before ocean liners were adequately gyroscoped. Only, instead of producing a green color and your breakfast, they will, *any second,* produce a volcanic eruption of uncontrollable, gut-busting, totally embarrassing laughter. Your spouse can feel you shaking. The whole row can feel you shaking. "Leave!" orders your spouse. You do so. And once outside the auditorium, with the door closed behind you, you burst into laughter. You choke, you drool, you roll your eyes. You hope they can't hear you inside.

Eventually the giddiness subsides, but you don't trust yourself to reenter the auditorium. So you wander the halls, which are lined with students' work: drawings, paintings, collages, some interesting masks made by shearing gallon milk containers in half and gluing stuff to them. One of them has Samuel Adams beer caps for eyes and curls made of "undone" cardboard toilet paper tubes.

Kids are doing such interesting things these days.

How To Turn Out
A Great Reader: A Recipe

To turn out a great reader, you will need the following four ingredients:

a) One ample lap easily accessible to a small child.

b) Proximity to a bookstore with a decent children's department.

c) A library card (preferably in the child's name).

d) An understanding that a love of books and reading is one of the greatest, grandest, and most valuable gifts you can bestow upon a child.

To bestow this precious gift you will need to follow certain steps.

1. *Begin Preparation Early* —While your three-month-old baby won't derive much literary value from being read to, your big-eyed bundle will get a great deal of pleasure and satisfaction out of the warm comfort of Mommy's or Daddy's lap, the dulcet or vibrant tones of Mommy's or Daddy's voice, and the fascinating effect of changing colors and shapes produced by turning pages.

At six months the benefits derived from reading to your baby will no longer be merely warm and cuddly. It will have become an important part of your child's learning experience. While it will be months before your child will be *producing* language, he or she has been *consuming* language every waking hour of the day. Of course, you have been talking to your baby virtually since birth and will continue to do so. Reading

to your baby—going slowly through a picture book pointing
to the objects and saying their names — is different. Point to
boat, say "boat." Point to truck, say "truck." This point-and-
say method will begin to do the very important job of helping
your child match certain sounds to certain objects, which is an
essential part of what language is about.

Though many kinds of books—board books, cloth books,
and bath books—are designed for the very young, almost any
book (or magazine) with pictures can be adapted to the point-
and-say method. There is a particular kind of board book that
is almost invariably a smash with babies. It consists simply of
photographs of babies. What they lack in variety they make up
for in "identification." Six-month-olds love them and they
adapt easily to the point-and-say method. You simply point to
the picture and say "baby!" Turn the page, point to the picture, and say, "baby!" Turn the page, point to the picture, and
say—you guessed it—"baby!"

2. *Stir in Additional Ingredients* — You will, of course,
continue to read to your child when he or she reaches the one-
to three-year-old plateau. All sorts of exciting things begin to
happen. Little pigs leave home, build houses of variously suitable materials, and run afoul of huffing-puffing wolves.
Certain individuals put in thumbs and pull out plums. Foolish
fellows act upon the notion that they can buy pies without any
penny. Daredevils risk a hot foot by leaping over flames.
Abusive husbands shut their wives up in gourds. (Question:
What did Peter Peter Pumpkin Eater say to his wife after
putting her in a pumpkin shell? Answer: Have a gourd day!)
Little girls with little curls suffer wild mood swings. (Another
question: Has Planned Parenthood ever thought of using the
Old Woman Who Lived in a Shoe as a poster person?)

Yes, it's a mad, mad, mad, mad world filled with excitement, conflict, suspense, and charismatic characters. The likes of Simon being simple, Jack being nimble, and Boy Blue falling asleep on the job are powerful stuff for little kids, fully as capable of entering their lives as a Shakespeare sonnet or Cole Porter song is of entering the lives of adults. The fact that even very young children can be deeply affected by literature is brought home to us by a professor of education at a nearby university. The experience she related had to do with her eighteen-month-old daughter and *Inside, Outside, Upside Down*, a book we wrote and illustrated some years ago. It tells the story of a little bear who crawls into a big box which is then hand-trucked outside and placed upside down on the bed of a pickup truck, which then heads for town. A bump causes the box to fall from the truck. The little bear emerges from the box and runs home shouting, "Mama! Mama! I went to town, inside, outside, upside down!" The book was intended to deal with the phenomenon of prepositional simultaneity and was designed as a prereader for four- to five-year-old children. Though the professor had bought the book for an older sibling, her eighteen-month-old daughter had adopted it as her own and from time to time required it to be read to her.

One morning the professor was called out of class to take an emergency call from the director of her daughter's day-care center. Her daughter, said the director, was behaving in a bizarre manner and, perhaps, might even be having some sort of a seizure. She was groveling into and trying to stand on her head in the toy box, all the while babbling and screaming for her mama.

The professor rushed over to the day-care center. Upon being told that her mother was coming, the child calmed down. But immediately upon seeing her mother, she again launched into her "seizure." And just as immediately her mother knew what her daughter was doing. She was acting out our book. Her babble wasn't babble at all. It was her ill-formed version of the little bear's triumphant finale, "Mama! Mama! I went to town, inside, outside, upside down!"

Somehow our little book—it has only thirty-two pages and contains only seventy-four words—had entered the consciousness of that little girl and become part of her being.

It shouldn't be surprising. There is a long history and powerful tradition of individuals being not only moved but moved to action by stories, poems, pieces of music, and paintings. Our failure to recognize that even very young children have rich inner lives subject to the full range of external stimuli is a kind of reverse ageism we would do well to guard against.

3. *Let Simmer While Continuing to Stir* — Provided you have managed to keep TV viewing time within reasonable bounds, there is a good chance that books and reading have become as much a part of your youngster's life as running, jumping, and climbing. It need hardly be said that family settings in which books and reading are a meaningful presence are much more likely to produce readers than those where channel surfing is the predominant family pursuit.

Slowly but surely your budding bibliophile has accumulated a not inconsiderable library. Its volumes range in condition from a mostly scotch tape *Green Eggs and Ham* to a mint-condition Richard Scarry ABC—the latter having been chosen just this morning from the supermarket spinner rack. Indeed, one of the reasons your youngster's collection is so large is your sweets-no/books-yes policy: While Junior may *not* get a sweet with every trip to the supermarket, he *may* take home a book each time. While it's not always an easy rule to make stick (indeed, it may even trigger an occasional head-banging fit at the checkout), it is nonetheless a policy worth pursuing. It will not only reduce the incidence of cavities in your child's teeth, but may also, unless the books chosen are completely mindless, reduce the incidence of cavities in your child's mind.

Plus, slowly and surely, and in ways too numerous and gradual to perceive, Junior will begin to make the connections that will allow him to perform the difficult and complicated decoding procedure we call reading. Perhaps "Sesame Street" will pitch in with its lively and entertaining phonics-based presentation of the letters of the alphabet. Their own names are powerfully evocative to children. Teaching a child to recognize and write "*STUART*" or "*CLOE*" is a potent demonstration of the power and value of reading.

While it's never a good idea to pressure or push a child to learn to read, it's perfectly okay to point out the presence of one or two letters of his own name in some larger text. He may find the idea that "his letters" are part of a vast, infinitely larger world of letters very exciting and go on a letter hunt. "Look! There's another! And another! And another!" Talk about excitement! Talk about information highway!

Or he may think it the most boring idea you've ever suggested. But that's okay. Different kids; different quids.

There are environmental factors that can help your child learn to read: signs, billboards, even graffiti.

"Hey, Dad," says Junior. "Who's this guy 'Nosmo King'?"

"Nosmo King? Nosmo King?" muses Dad. "Never heard of him."

"Well, his name's all over the place," says Junior, pointing to the twelfth No Smoking sign he's seen that day.

For most children, learning to read is a catch-as-catch-can

combination of connecting the dots and trying to assemble a thousand-piece jigsaw puzzle that's mostly sky. You connect a few dots here and a few dots there. You find some sky that meets a horizon and gradually the big picture begins to emerge.

There are children, however, who at a very early age learn to read virtually overnight, almost, it seems, without trying. The extreme range of difference in the aptitude for and the attitude toward learning to read is exemplified by two children of friends of ours. When we heard that little Max, age two, had taught himself to read, we were dubious. His parents read the disbelief in our expression and offered a kind of "take a card, any card at all" demonstration. "Give him something to read," they said, "anything at all!" An equally dubious fellow guest tendered little Max a matchbook from a local establishment. He took the matchbook in hand and, Kreskin-like, read, "The Venice Restaurant, fine food and wines; call for reservations; ask about our banquet facilities." Then, squinting at some fine print, he read, "Please close before striking."

Max's older brother, Howie, on the other hand, was rather intimidated by the prospect of having to learn to read. At one point, when he was about four, his mother had been reading him *The Wind in the Willows* one chapter at a time at bedtime. One evening, after slipping off his mom's lap, he turned and took the book from her. He opened it and looked at the rows and rows of type. After a long pause, he looked up at his mom and said, "You know something? Even after I learn to read, I don't think I'm going to be able to do it."

Of course, he did learn to do it. And very well. In fact, by the time each of the boys reached third grade, their reading scores were identical, and later, when they took their SATs, their verbals were a scant ten points apart.

Controversy and anxiety about kids learning to read has been continuous and rife for decades. A thriving reading-aids industry has grown up and fastened itself on that anxiety. The products offered divide into two general categories: specially designed easy-to-read book programs, usually sold through mail solicitation, and sets of audio- and/or videotapes stressing phonics. These programs vary considerably and should be sampled for quality, efficacy, and cost before purchase. The book programs tend to be less expensive and more readily sampled. The audio tape programs, which are sold through TV and radio advertising, tend to be more expensive and less readily sampled.

Most schools employ a mixed approach to the teaching of the first "R." They combine the teaching of phonics (the sounding out of words based on phonetic letter sounds) with the "word method"(which stresses recognition of whole words). A relatively new approach called the "whole language" method is being added to the mix. This method employs carefully selected "trade books"(the kind of children's books available from bookstores and libraries) instead of basal readers.

The ability to read is so extraordinarily important to success and even survival in modern society that a certain amount of parental anxiety about kids learning to read is not surprising. But if through the years you've managed to find the time and energy to read to your baby, your toddler, and your tot, you can be reasonably sure that come first grade, your child will be reading to you.

4. *Season to Taste (Your Child's Taste)* — For a number of years during the early seventies, there was a ubiquitous fellow named Charlie Tuna who was virtually unavoidable on the tube. It was Charlie's role as a spokesfish for Star-Kist to show

up sartorially splendid in an underwater setting into which a worm-laden fishhook had just descended. When Charlie, whose dream was to become the contents of a Star-Kist tuna can, shot his cuffs, adjusted his weskit, and straightened his tie preparatory to taking the hook, a voice was heard.

"Sorry, Charlie," said the voice. "Star-Kist doesn't want tunas with good taste. Star-Kist wants tunas that taste good."

So it is with kids who, having labored long and hard, have finally managed to learn to read. They don't want books with good taste; they want books that taste good! The last thing your youngster needs at a time when he or she is beginning to feel some sense of autonomy is to be told which friends to choose, what clothes to wear, what music to listen to—and which books to read.

Of course you want your youngster to be exposed to the classics, to appreciate fine literature. But don't fret if his or her taste runs to popular series, comic books, and tales from the crypt. The important thing is that your child is reading!

So whatever sort of reading habit your child develops, encourage and support it! Hey, you grew up on the Hardy Boys, Nancy Drew, *Mad* magazine, and the jokes that came on bubblegum wrappers, and look how wonderfully discriminating, cultured, and classy you turned out.

Two-Wheeler Tip

Most kids learn to ride a two-wheeled bike fairly readily, though not without a certain amount of wear and tear on the instructor, who, more often than not, is Daddy.

In point of fact, there are few parental pursuits more frazzling than running hunched over, holding on to a youngster astride a wobbling bike, shouting breathless encouragements like, "Keep pedaling, dammit! Keep pedaling!" Most youngsters manage to learn this way. They find their balance and are turned loose to experience the thrill of two-wheeled locomotion. But not before Daddy is reduced to a state of shaken exhaustion and consigned to his La-Z-Boy, where he sits sucking disconsolately on a double Johnny Walker.

But some youngsters, perhaps frightened, perhaps distracted by seeing their nice Dr. Jekyll daddy transmogrify into a sweating, swearing Mr. Hyde, just don't seem to be able to get the hang of a two-wheeler.

After watching her daughter crash a couple of times, a mother we know decided that a team-teaching approach might be the better part of her husband's valor and her daughter's cuts and bruises.

She set up the following teaching arrangement: Daddy stands beside and slightly to the rear of the two-wheeler, firmly propping up bike and child. Mother positions herself a few feet away in a confidence-inspiring catching position. Then, simultaneously with the order to pedal, Daddy gives the bike a strong push toward Mother.

The process is repeated with the distance between launcher and catcher gradually increasing. Before long, even the most laggard learner will ride joyously into the wild asphalt yonder.

Preparing Your Child for Those Difficult First-Time Experiences—A Checklist

A little sensible preventative information on difficult first-time experiences can not only save you and your child a certain amount of upset, but may even head off a few galloping traumas at the pass.

1. *Try to Put Yourself in Your Child's Shoes and Look at Each First-Time Experience from Your Child's Point of View —*

It's obvious that youngsters need some preparation for such troublesome experiences as visiting the doctor or dentist, or such major, life-changing developments as starting school or moving to a new neighborhood. But, if you examine prospective new experiences

critically, you may find that even "fun" places and events can be upsetting. The fact that a movie house is dark, for example, is taken for granted by adults, but it could come as a disconcerting shock to an unprepared tot. The roaring reality of lions and tigers at the zoo is very different from the cuddly camaraderie of the stuffed lions and tigers little children sleep with.

2. *Don't Lie* — If you hear yourself saying, "It won't hurt, sweetie!" bite your tongue. Always tell your children as much of the truth as they can understand, if not out of a fundamental moral imperative, then at least in an effort to establish and maintain the most valuable attribute you have as a parent—your credibility. If you con your three-year-old into believing that the booster shot won't hurt, why should he or she believe your later claims that marijuana, booze, and skipping school will?

3. *Avoid the "Hard Sell"*— Overselling a first-time experience is almost inevitably counterproductive. Telling a youngster he or she is going to "just love" kindergarten, for example, is bound to arouse suspicion and skepticism. A better approach is simply to tell your youngster what's going to happen in kindergarten—that there will be other children, special blocks to play with, a barrel of modeling clay, paints and crayons, all sorts of things to make and do, and a teacher who will be in charge. Generally speaking, young children like the idea that someone will be in charge. A visit to the kindergarten classroom in advance of the first-time experience is very much in order if it can be arranged.

4. *Don't Negotiate* — Don't get into a negotiation with your child on a matter of necessity. If your youngster senses that you feel guilty or overly anxious about taking him for a shot, or a dental exam, or to kindergarten, your efforts to prepare him for the experience will create more problems than they will solve. Going to the doctor, the dentist, or school is not negotiable.

5. *Know Your Child* — Perhaps the most important thing to remember in dealing with children is that no two of them are alike. Advice and handy-dandy rules (like these) are useful only if you adapt them to the needs of your particular child. There *are* children who are so sturdy (or insensitive) that they need very little preparation for anything, and there are those at the other extreme who need a scenario at every turn of the road. But most kids fall into that middle range that includes most of us—individuals who would like to have some idea just what the heck is going to happen next.

Oh, How They Forget!

Our grandniece, Alexandra, a doll-like two-year-old with a head of wonderfully curly blond hair, came home from nursery school one day and informed her mother that some of the other mommies had told her she looked just like Shirley Temper. Her mother was delighted, of course. But before she could fully savor the lovely compliment, Alex asked, "Who's Shirley Temper?"

Why Is It That . . .

. . . when playing games, children who cannot perceive that you are cheating outrageously in their favor when they are young won't give you the least little break when you've lost a few steps?

Toy Evaluation (Advanced Course)

Since play is your child's work, it is necessary to approach the process of toy evaluation with seriousness of purpose. Here is a set of cautionary criteria that should be applied when evaluating any toy you may contemplate purchasing for your child.

1. If it requires batteries, determine whether they are available a) in the immediate vicinity, b) in the state, c) in the U.S. of A., d) on the immediate planet.

2. Does it have so many parts that picking up its pieces will send you to the chiropractor?

3. In the event that its pieces are not all picked up, will it hurt if you step on one in your bare feet in the dark? (Or, similarly, if it's a bath toy, will it hurt if you sit on it in the bathtub?)

4. If left out in the rain for forty-eight hours, will it lose any substantial part of its play value?

5. Does it fall into the treacherous category of TV-advertised toys which carry the barely visible line EACH COMPONENT SOLD SEPARATELY?

6. Does it have sufficient play value to pull your youngster away from the tube for more than four minutes?

7. If sound is part of its appeal, will the noise it produces drive you over the edge?

8. Does it throw up, urinate, lactate, or give birth?

9. Does it appeal excessively to your child's natural affinity for things slimy, gooey, or otherwise disgusting?

If the toy under consideration passes muster on all of the above nine counts and does not cost more than $129.99 (and the mall Santa promised it to your kid anyway), you may as well hand over your credit card to the checkout person and go quietly with your purchase.

The Good News and Bad News About Television

As with so many things parents have to deal with, television is a good news/bad news situation. The good news about television in the early years of parenting is that it's a perfectly marvelous babysitter. Television's ability to grab the eyeballs of your terrible two, threatening three, feisty four, or fearsome five and hold on to them long enough for you to get a little R and R (nothing ambitious—just  a few minutes staring at the ceiling with your feet up) makes television a boon and a blessing to be preserved and treasured.

The bad news about television is that it's a perfectly terrible babysitter. Television's ability to lobotomize your little spud into a full-blown couch potato who is all eyes and no brain makes it a clear and present danger to your child's becoming president or much of anything else.

Television, as it presents itself today, is a pretty good example of Shakespeare's concept of "outrageous fortune," except that "TV or not TV" is hardly the question. Television is not only here to stay, it's proliferating, not to say metastisizing, at such a rate that Ray Bradbury's prophetic vision of a totally TV-dominated society in which the very walls of our homes have become TV screens, may come to pass.

But prophetic visions aside, how does a parent strike a balance between the good news and the bad news about television? Our answer: *very carefully.*

Here are some thoughts and ideas on how to be careful about your child's television watching.

1. *TV and Mother's Milk* —Many if not most children first experience television out of the corner of an eye when they are nursing or taking formula. While it's perfectly understandable that an overextended mom would wish to simply "go blank" and watch Oprah or Phil during the endlessly repetitious task of feeding, it is not necessarily advisable. Though there is no body of evidence that the association of TV and mother's milk will turn Junior into a TV junkie, there is a considerable body of evidence that feeding time is a very special time of bonding and communion between mother and child, best observed without benefit of Oprah or Phil.

2. *How Much? How Soon?* —While there are exceptions to almost every generalization about two-year-olds, it is fair to say that most two-year-olds will sit still for quite a lot of television.

That's the problem.

The reason it's a problem is that one of the things a two-year-old least needs is TV. What two-year-olds need is to get on with their lives. They need to run, jump, climb, dance, and spin till they drop. They need to go through a hunter/gatherer stage. They need to know, for example, that thousand-leggers taste awful; that ants, while they smell like grape soda, taste worse than thousand-leggers; that dust devils, while attractive and easy to catch, make you choke. Two-year-olds need to become socialized. They need to begin constructing a model of the real world. They need to know that if you bite a sibling, the sibling will bite back; that Mommy is always good for a hug; that Daddy is almost always good for a tickle; that Gramps and Gran are always good for hugs, kisses, tickles, and lots of presents.

How much television, how soon?

A half hour a day is plenty for a two-year-old. What's best for your small viewer to watch? Of the PBS range of shows— "Sesame Street," "Shining Time Station," "Mr. Rogers," "Barney"—it hardly matters. Except it should be the child's choice—even if it is "Barney." If Barney bugs you, work on overcoming those Bad Barney Feelings. Relax, loosen your choler, go into another room.

3. *The Bad News Gets Worse* —Long before our eponymous bears were even a gleam in our eye, we contributed a monthly cartoon feature to *McCall's* magazine. It evolved into a sort of graphic sitcom in which some circumstance of family life was covered in a series of cartoons. The feature attracted the attention of the late Joyce C. Hall, founder and chairman of Hallmark cards. Mr. Hall invited us to Kansas City, the home of Hallmark, to discuss the use of our characters in Hallmark greeting products. The invitation included a stay at a penthouse apartment Hallmark maintained for visitors. We were informed we would be sharing that apartment, which

turned out to be vast, magnificent, and fully staffed, with some visitors from England. To our surprise and delight, our fellow guests were Roland and Mary Emmet, he of *Punch* and the marvelously funny and intensely British train cartoons for which he was famous.

We became instantaneously friendly over a butler-served tea. Immediately upon the butler's departure to the pantry, the Emmets turned serious. They looked furtively from side to side like characters in a spy movie.

"I don't know quite how to say this, Stan and Jan," said Roland, leaning forward and pointing at the television, "but did you know that there are commercials for *toilet tissue* on the telly?"

Oh, if the Emmets could see our telly now! Not only toilet tissue, but animated rolls of the stuff chatting up attractive lady seatmates in an airline setting, bragging about extra softness; beer commercials featuring scantily clad, buxom, blond beauties descending out of the sky into various male enclaves; English Leather pitches so sensual that they would make I AM CURIOUS YELLOW blush; a virtual Olympic competition of toilet-bowl cleaners; and an endless succession of sullen sex kittens breathlessly imploring you to call *their* 900 number.

And these are just the commercials. The "entertainment" portion of television piles on with thousands of shootings, stabbings, garrotings, torturings, beatings, rapes, and incinerations.

TV continues to be a good news/bad news situation as the parenting experience proceeds apace, except that the bad news gets much worse.

A case in point to demonstrate how much worse. When our kids were young, the worst juvenile behavior model available on the tube was Eddie Haskell, a regular on "Leave It to

Beaver." About the worst things Eddie ever did was accuse Beaver and Wally of being Goody Two-shoes and suggest that perhaps grown-ups didn't have a monopoly on the world's wisdom. It's quite a plummet from mildly miscreant Eddie Haskell to today's bad dudes, the terminally vulgar and criminally callow Beavis and Butthead, whose preoccupations are bodily functions, products, and sounds, and whose activities have included pyromania and cat torture.

Since child pornography is, thus far, the only area where children's rights have successfully prevailed over First Amendment rights, it's going to continue to be up to parents to keep track of what their kids are watching on television.

Not that the effect of TV can be measured with precision. It's more a matter of watching for signs and symptoms and titrating the dose accordingly. If, for example, four-year-old Donny starts trying to run through walls superhero style, you might check out what Saturday-morning cartoons he's been watching; if six-year-old Darla starts expressing herself in icky-poo baby talk, you might consider reducing her intake of Lamb Chop; if nine-year-old Ned starts going around saying everything "sucks," you may have to cut out "The Simpsons."

But what do you do when twelve-year-old Greg adopts the forbidden Beavis and Butthead's cretinous cackle—a clear sign that he's watching those worthies at some other venue?

There's not a heckuva lot you *can* do, except, perhaps, console yourself with the idea that all the good work you did during those early "input" years will inoculate your youngster against the infectious vulgarity of outrageous television.

4. *MTV—There's the Rub* — And what a lot of rubbery thrusting, wriggly rubbing it is! All of it lubricious, lascivious, and lovingly produced. All of it accompanied by lyrics of lust

and longing. All of it targeted at vulnerable, sexually insecure teens. All of it expertly and artfully crafted to increase the incidence of teen sex and thus its cataclysmic consequences: children having children, the cessation of education by young females who desperately need it, the increasing incidence of AIDS among teens.

The decision whether to come down hard, easy, or in-between on the likes of MTV depends on how impressionable, how needy, how mature, and how well grounded a youngster is.

Many, if not most, parents consider MTV close to being an Unmitigated Evil and deal with it summarily for as long as they can without triggering open rebellion. But there are exceptions to every rule—even the Rule of Unmitigated Evil. In the interest of equal time, a contrary case in point: a friend of ours who is the mother of a fairly typical twelve-year-old daughter decided that the swinging style of the high-intensity suburban middle school her daughter was attending was a little scary. After considerable soul-searching, she took her out of the swinging middle school and put the girl in a religious school of the family's persuasion. But there was an unanticipated result. The youngster came under the influence of an extremely ascetic teacher who turned her away from her hitherto swinging ways: The girl not only became an ascetic herself, she became vociferously critical of her parents' highly "immoral" life-style, which includes moderate social drinking, occasionally saying "damn" and "hell," and watching HBO. This turn of events became a fairly serious family problem, with our friend beginning to become concerned that she would lose her daughter to some rigorously abnegating religious order.

Some time after being told about the situation, we asked how the "problem" with her daughter was going.

"My fingers are tightly crossed," said the mother, "but I

think that maybe she's getting over it. At least I hope to God she is!"

We asked what was happening to make her think so.

"Well," she answered, heaving a great sigh of relief, "She's starting to watch MTV again."

Why Is It That . . .

. . . those same children who consider repetition (ad infinitum) the soul of wit when they are young, grow up to be individuals who consider the least little retelling of a parent's favorite story an unmistakable sign of the onset of senility ("Daddy! You've told me that story before!")?

Air Travel with Children

The thought that comes initially to mind when considering an advisory with respect to air travel with children is DON'T.

But with family and friends becoming more and more widely separated, air travel with children becomes the only alternative to not seeing sister Sue in Dubuque, brother Bill in Michigan's upper peninsula, or Great Uncle Roy in Net Worth, Texas—oops, Fort Worth, Texas. No need to blush. Uncle Roy *is* rich, and he *does* love the kids. Since we can't expect you to "just say no" to air travel with children, we feel conscience- and duty-bound to let you know what you're in for—and to take our best shot at being helpful.

1. *Beware of the Airport* — Airports are such exhilarating places that kids tend to run wild in them—or even amuck. It's no wonder. Airports offer such attractive hazards as giant life-threatening escalators, high-speed people movers, hurtling

electric vehicles that come *beep-beep*ing down on you from all directions, and crowds, crowds, crowds! So it's important to keep your brood together lest any of your chicks stray, get lost, or get run over.

2. *Souvenir and Vending-Machine Policy* — Airport managements provide numerous terminal gift and souvenir shops offering terminally overpriced gifts and souvenirs, as well as candy and drink machines as far as the eye can see.

Forewarn your little consumers of this state of affairs. Explain that you're going on a *trip,* not a *shopping* trip. Explain further that the purpose of a souvenir is to remind you of where you've been, not where you already are. Assure them that they will be permitted to buy souvenirs on the way home from your visit to Aunt Sue, Uncle Bill, or Great Uncle Roy. As for gifts for your hosts, you've already bought those at the local mall.

You should also lay down the law with respect to candy and drink machines. Remind your group that they've just had lunch and, further, that you've got plenty of snacks in your carry-on baggage for in-flight consumption. As for drinks, the purpose of proscribing them should be obvious: toileting small children in flight is difficult at best—at worst, during a severely bumpy stretch, for example, it's roughly equivalent to going over Niagara Falls in a barrel.

3. *A Preboarding Checklist* —You have run the airport gauntlet without losing any of your party or going broke, and arrived at gate 34B (the next to the last gate on the longest concourse in the airport). You stake out a likely campsite in the boarding area and go through the Standard Air Travel with Children checklist (see page 102).

a) Locate the Men's and Ladies' nearest the boarding area and enforce the everybody-has-to-go-to-the-bathroom-before-we-get-on-the-airplane rule. If Daddy or anyone else says, "I don't hafta," he or she is to be hustled in a firm but friendly manner into the facility "to try."

b) Your various totes, carryalls, and overnights should be reordered and recompacted so as to have a better chance of passing the increasingly strict carry-on rule: Nothing that cannot fit under the seat in front of you or be stored in an overhead compartment.

c) Check for the skeenteenth time to see if the tickets are where you thought they were.

d) Point out to your kids that you are close to boarding and that *nobody* is to wander away from the boarding area under *any circumstances*. It's up to you whether to tell them that the homeless people they've noticed are folk who got left behind as kids and have been wandering the airport ever since.

e) Proudly watch Daddy collapse the collapsible stroller for the last time before boarding. Daddy's come a long way since those early practice sessions in the garage.

f) Pass out tickets, baggage, and hand-holding assignments and listen for the early-boarding announcement from the podium.

4. *Early Boarding* — All airlines allow early boarding of passengers who are traveling with children. By all means take advantage of this privilege. It is advisable, also, given the incomprehensibility of some boarding area public address systems, to hedge your bets by moving close to the boarding gate so that you're ready to rumble when the action starts.

And let's give our much-maligned airline friends credit for

giving families a slight edge. True, it's just good business to do so. But it's not true, as has been suggested by some airline watch groups, that early boarding is really just a sharp practice designed to get wavering passengers onto the aircraft before they come to their senses and run screaming from the airport.

5. *Up and Away* — Let's establish at the outset that the cramped, crowded interior of an airliner is a very difficult environment for children. It depends on the age and nature of the child and on the duration of the flight, of course, but most kids do not get a kick out of air travel. They tend to agree with the lyric that states that ". . . flying up high/ with some guy in the sky/ is my i-dea/ of nothing to do. . . ." There are some flight- and space-oriented kids—usually, but not always, boys—who are excellent air travelers. They are fascinated by the incredible acceleration of jet takeoff, knowledgeable about the clunk of the landing gear retracting, interested in the operation of the ailerons, and attentive to the flight attendant's safety presentation. But such kids are the exception rather than the rule. Most kids figure out pretty quickly that the modern airliner, which looks so interesting from the outside—landing, taking off, taxiing, displaying its snazzy logo—is, from a passenger's point of view, just a big boring old bus with wings. They figure out pretty early in the flight that this big exciting adventure they've been promised is in reality just a long wait.

And to add insult to disappointment, they strap you in, forbid you to kick the seat in front of you, prevent you from standing up in your seat and staring over the seat-back at the people behind you, and stop you from pushing any of the seat-buttons that just cry out for pushing. As for the view, once you've seen one cloud, you've seen them all. It's not only a wait, it's a bloody long boring wait. It's no wonder kids begin twitching, writhing, whimpering, chafing, and grousing even before the seatbelt light goes off.

How do you prepare for the exigencies of air travel with children? The same way you prepare for any of the long waits you inevitably encounter in the course of your duties as a parent: You stock up on "sit still" items.

Inexpensive coloring and activity books are the most obvious "sit still" items. Given the circumstances, you might want to employ a "forbidden fruit" strategy. In the case of your four-year-old son, it might mean coming up with coloring books featuring the sort of action-oriented licensed TV characters you wouldn't normally give houseroom to. "Gee, Mom," says your strapped-in little fellow traveler, *"Power Rangers* and *X-men!* You said I couldn't have those."

Perhaps you've been trying to convince your seven-year-old daughter that she's too big for Barbie. (We can't understand why, Mom—you've still got *your* collection.) A clutch of Barbie coloring books may set the weaning process back a bit, but won't it be worth it to see her clam happy in "Barbie heaven" for most of the flight?

A big brand-new box of crayons to go with the coloring books makes a fine adjunct treat. (Never mind that you have lots of perfectly adequate crayons at home. We're talking about *air travel with children!)*

For older kids, sliding-number tray puzzles are good, as are those extraordinarily difficult puzzles that consist of two bent interlocking lengths of stainless steel that only preteens can get apart. A 3-D Viewmaster with lots of new discs is fun for all. But you get the idea.

What *not* to take along on an airplane: any toy or activity that requires a larger field of operation than the fold-down dining tray. Also, need we say, avoid anything with lots of little bits, like jigsaw puzzles or Legos. An in-flight Lego fight among your children is not what you're looking for.

Speaking of dining: Since kids tend to be archconservatives when it comes to food, and given the fact that airline food doesn't *look* like any other food your child has seen, it's possible that your child won't want any part of it, except perhaps for the toasted nuts and the chocolate chip cookies. That's why you brought lots of tried and true kid food along: Cheerios, rice cakes, peanut butter and jelly, and any other kind of sandwich your kids may be addicted to. Drinks are no problem on airlines. Or *should* we say, drinks are plentiful on airlines. There's always milk, in those little unopenable square boxes. Resolutely ignore protestations of "I do it myself," no matter how vociferous.

Intake of liquids, of course, results in outgo of liquids. As we suggested earlier, toileting small children on airplanes is no day at the beach, though you may find yourself awash underfoot occasionally. It's not that kids aren't interested in bathroom matters. The problem is that space is limited on planes, and lavatory space is so brutally limited that accompanying a small child into the compartment, we cannot resist repeating, is roughly equivalent to going over that famous falls in a barrel—a steel barrel.

Many small children find the airplane lavatory experience very interesting. They like the blue water that flows when you flush. They like it when the airplane hits a big airbump and Daddy knocks his coconut on the bulkhead.

Older kids who have become accustomed to the boys room/girls room dichotomy of school and other institutions, find the unisex aspect of the airline facilities intriguing.

Other, more logistically minded kids ask, "What happens to it, Dad?" In most cases a simple explanation of the principal of chemical toilets will suffice. But, hark! Your captain just instructed the flight attendants to prepare for landing.

After scurrying up and down the aisle collecting cups and checking seatbelts and seat-backs, they belt themselves into their little jump seats and down you trend.

"Look, Dad!" shouts Junior, "the wing is coming apart!" "No, son," explains Dad, "those are the wing flaps. They reduce lift and slow the plane down so—" But Dad is interrupted by the screams of younger brother and sister. "My ears hurt! My ears hurt!" Again Mother is prepared. She whips out chunks of Bloney Gum (another normally forbidden fruit). "Here, chew on this. It will equalize the pressure in your ears." It won't quite, but it does help.

Now you're through the clouds. You can see ground, and you feel that special endorphin high that only parents feel. You got through it!

Happy landing . . . .

And say "Hi" to sister Sue, brother Bill, or Great Uncle Roy.

Why Is It That . . .

. . . the more precariously you lean over so as to hear what children are saying, the more inaudibly they speak?

How To Deal with the Showdown at Generation Gap

Of all the trials and tribulations of parenting, none is more disheartening than that feeling of frustration and helplessness we encounter when our reasonably manageable, occasionally lovable children turn almost overnight into largely unmanageable, mostly unlovable teens.

Though there is no way to turn the rocky, twisting road of parent/teen relations into a straight, smooth, well-marked highway, it is possible to avoid some of the more dangerous potholes, sinkholes, and cave-ins.

Here are some forewarnings.

1. *It's Different Now* —The teen years have always been a time of trouble between the generations. It wouldn't surprise us in the least, for example, if some newly discovered time capsule were to reveal that young George Washington chopped down that cherry tree in a fit of pique because his dad wouldn't let him have the horse that night. And further, that he not only didn't confess to the act, but blamed it on some neighbor kid across the Rappahannock.

It is true enough that generational conflict, with its baggage of anger, stress, frustration, and disappointment, has come down to us through the ages pretty much intact. It is also true that the older generation's need to maintain control and the need of the younger generation to break free of that control remains the underlying cause of the conflict.

But this is not to say that the more things change, the more they remain the same. The teen world that tilts and whirls around us today is materially and radically different. So as you enter the eddies of generational conflict, bear in mind that it's different now—and worse. Worse for teens and, consequently, worse for parents.

2. *Why Is It Worse?* — Part of the reason is that while the teen years have always been troubled ones, only relatively recently have high-powered marketers of sex- and violence-saturated movies, TV, music, video games, apparel, footwear, cosmetics, and almost any other product you can imagine been going after teen dollars with such rapacious gusto. This head-long grab for a share of teens' disposable income has a serious, even tragic downside: disposable teens.

There is no tomorrow for the thousands of teens who have been lost to the tender mercies of our sex- and violence-ridden media culture. Increasingly, teen lives are being destroyed by premature, indiscriminate sex—HIV infection and AIDS have reached almost epidemic proportions among teens—and suicide, which the press reminds us of almost daily, has recently joined murder as a leading cause of death among teens.

And those are just the products that can be legally marketed and sold to teens. What about tobacco products and beer, which, while they can't be legally *sold* to teens, are marketed to them with great zeal. Now the tobacco companies are even going after preteens. If you doubt that's the case, may we remind you of that tot-to-teen idol Joe Camel, who has as high a recognition rating among children as Mickey Mouse.

Nor are occasional public-service announcements cautioning against underage drinking likely to persuade sexually insecure teens to ignore the endless parade of lubricious beer commercials which hammer home the proposition that beer is a veritable cupid's elixir when it comes to bringing boys and girls together.

3. *Different Teens, Different Means* — What are parents to do to get their kids through the increasingly turbulent and difficult teen years? Part of the answer is that if parents have set a reasonably good example and set forth a reasonably serviceable set of values, they've already done much of what they can do. Though it may not seem so in the heat of battle, most teens care deeply about their parents' opinion of them and the way they are conducting their lives. This influence may be vestigial, tenuous, even unconscious, but it's there, and it's one of the best things parents have going for them during this difficult period.

Though teens are all teens together, they are as different one from the other as they were when they were tots. There are bold teens, shy teens, independent teens, clinging teens, teens who are already on clear career paths, teens who aren't even thinking about tomorrow, mall teens, nerd teens, jock teens, sex-obsessed teens, teens who are scared of their own sexual shadow. And they all need to be understood and dealt with as individuals—each according to his or her needs, as it were.

This is not to say, however, that there are no stratagems that can be generally applied. Herewith, some painfully arrived at ones that may help you weather your particular teen's stormy rite of passage.

a) Do not be put off by your teen's persistent and vociferous tendency to say "Mo-ther!" or "Daddy, please!" in response to such neutral remarks as "Looks like rain" or "Hi!"

b) Maintain the position that your teen is still an integral part of the family and take his or her interests and enthusiasms into account when planning family events, outings, trips, and vacations.

c) Insist upon reasonable curfews, but allow for some selective flexibility.

d) Adopt and apply former president Reagan's favorite Russian proverb, "Trust, but verify."

e) Volunteering your services as a chauffeur is an effective, nonprying way of knowing where your teen is at least some of the time.

f) Respect your teen's privacy. One thing a teen will never forgive is the rifling of his or her room under the excuse, "I was just trying to straighten up a little."

4. *Accept the Fact That Your Teen Holds the High Cards* — While you hold some pretty good hole cards—cards like "love," "patience," "wisdom," and "experience"—in any teen-parent showdown, it's your teen that holds the really high cards—such as "total withdrawal," "going the drug route," and "disappearing from the face of the earth." Since your object is to keep the game going, to maintain the connection, you are at a serious disadvantage. Your troubled teen can end the game simply by playing one of his or her cards. Your preferred strategy is to keep your cards in reserve (your teen knows that you have them) and not force whatever issue has precipitated the blowup of the moment.

5. *Earrings, Pigtails, and Other Distractions* — Most teens are willing to protect their parents from the knowledge that they are smoking, drinking, and having sex, but will resist to the death any attempt on the part of the parents to tell them how they should dress or wear their hair.

Despite the fact that they are essentially harmless, it's such fashion and style statements that trigger some of the most destructive teen-parent blowups. A statement, if you find it absolutely necessary, that you are not exactly crazy about your son's new earring-and-pigtail look is by far the better part of valor than going ballistic and precipitating a family crisis.

Except in the case of seriously self-destructive behavior, dealing with teens is essentially a holding action. The goal is for both parent and teen to get through it without any permanent damage. And speaking of seriously self-destructive behavior, a reasonably well-grounded teen who, because of peer pressure or the natural teen propensity for risk taking, is on the verge of serious trouble, is much more likely to bring his or her problem to a parent who has not gone ballistic over the likes of earrings or pigtails.

6. *Every Hurricane Has an Eye* — Every hurricane, including the hurricane called the parent-teen relationship, has an eye. A hurricane's eye is a small area of calm and quiet at the center of the raging storm. In the case of the hurricane that is the natural environment of most teens, the eye is a fleeting stretch of psychological space that somehow permits a troubled teen to open up to a parent. Should you find yourself in such a space, take advantage of it. It's unlikely to last. The raging storm may resume just as abruptly as it ceased. Push yourself to a higher level of parental percipience. Listen for your teen's dear life: He or she has come to you for help, not recriminations, I-told-you-so's, or shocked disbelief. Whatever is revealed to you, take it as seriously as your youngster obviously does. Don't be relieved if your teen's trouble has to do with a love relationship; remember: Romeo and Juliet's tragic demise was a case of "puppy love." Whatever it is—drugs, a pregnancy caused or incurred, school failure, concern about sexual identity, or depression—assure your teen of your unconditional support. Assure your son or daughter that whatever the problem is, you are there to help in any way he or she wants to be helped: by keeping it in the family, by seeking counseling, by changing schools—whatever it takes. Then follow up on whatever course seems appropriate. Follow up quietly, patiently, sensitively—and thank your lucky star that the eye of the hurricane found you.

A mother who was discouraged about her three-year-old's failure to become fully toilet trained sought advice from her pediatrician. The good doctor responded with some general advice about a reduction of pressure, some special advice about a change of approach, then, in an attempt to reassure the mother, said, "Things will work out. After all, she won't be in diapers in college." The troubled mother had a twofold problem with the doctor's comment: one, the doctor had set up a discouragingly long perspective, and two, what made him so sure the kid *wouldn't* be wearing diapers in college?

While it is perfectly natural for a parent to feel dissatisfied with child-rearing advice that does not prescribe a definite, concrete coarse of action, such advice is often the best that can be offered. Just as your three-year-old won't be a three-year-old forever, your teen won't be a teen forever. Your goal must be for you and your teen to get through the experience without serious permanent damage — and, if possible, with a minimum of screaming and hollering, Sturm und Drang, and blood on the floor.

The Seven Immutable Laws of Parent-Teen Interaction

(To be carved in the facade of the unlikely to-be-erected "Eight is Enough" Hall of Fame)

1. The Law of Intergenerational Listening — Teen willingness to listen varies inversely with the desperation of parental need to be heard and vice versa.

2. The Law of Teen Blamelessness —Teen blamelessness approaches zero as the enormity of teen error approaches infinity.

3. The Law of Generational Conflict —The intensity of generational conflict varies directly with the triviality of the point at issue.

4. The Law of the Divine Right of Parents— Likelihood of the assertion of the Divine Right of Parents approaches infinity as the tenability of the parent's position approaches zero.

5. The Law of Higher Education — Parental determination to get Junior into Harvard varies directly with the rate of Junior's inexorable drift toward Punxsutawney State.

6. The Law of Parental Snooping — Interest in the intimate affairs of teens increases as the affairs of teens become more intimate.

7. The Law of Volcanic Eruption —The probability of Father blowing his top at any given moment is precisely equal to the probability of his blowing his top at any other given moment.

The Greeks May Have Had a Word for It—But We Don't

Though it's not our prime intention
To precipitate a fuss,
It has upon reflection
Occurred repeatedly to us
That the rich and varied language
Known familiarly as English

Has not a solitary word
Which does in any way distinguish
Between the darling little children
Nature grants to us on loan
And the hulks that they become
When they are fully grown.

We do have many terms,
Like "adult children" and the like,
Which without a question
Describe a grown-up, not a tyke,
But they are oxymorons
And leave a lot to be desired
In identifying the vintage
Of the issue we have sired.

Why is it that there's not
Some term of Art or Nature
To fill this glaring gap
In parental nomenclature?

Perhaps the gods of language
Decided on their own
That there shouldn't be a word
For children who are grown,
That our children are our children,
No matter they grow gray,
That our children are our children
Forever and a day.

Mom Power

How are moms powerful? Let us count the ways. They are powerful when we are wee and colicky and only their warm comforting gets us through the night. They are powerful as we go through the endless sequence of shots, shots, and more shots and we know through our tears and pain that they are there. They are powerful when we are four and come home with a bloody nose inflicted by some five-year-old hulk of a bully and what we need are hugs, not marching orders from Dad to go right back out there and knock that kid's block off. They are powerful in concert with other moms, at the dangerous corner of Fourth and Elm, demanding the installation of a much-needed traffic light. They are powerful through our teen years when we are struggling to break free and it's only thoughts of Mom that keep us on the relatively straight and reasonably narrow.

And they are powerful when we are fully grown and need to be taken down a peg. As recently happened after a hard-fought NBA semifinal between the Chicago Bulls and the New York Knicks. A towering, glowering Knicks forward, who has been described by Bulls forward Scottie Pippin as the strongest man in basketball, had descended to the private Madison Square Garden garage where the players park their Ferraris, Mercedes, and Corvettes. His mother, who is about half her son's size, was with him. Some savvy kids had infiltrated this sanctum sanctorum in quest of autographs. The massive star forward, who had just played forty bruising minutes of "in the paint" basketball, was understandably not in the mood for kids clamoring for autographs.

But his mom understood differently. In no uncertain terms

she reminded her son that as a man who was once an autograph-seeking child himself, he had "obligations." So the clamoring kids got their autographs—because of Mom Power.

Children's Letters
to Stan, Jan, and the Berenstain Bears

One of the advantages of our day job is the letters we receive from kids and the insights they afford us into the hearts and minds of children far beyond our family circle.

Some of them are autobiographical.

8/12/84

Dear Stan + Jan,
My name is Billy. I am 8 years old and in 3rd grade in Hefenan School. I have 2 sisters and 2 dogs. My dad is named Bill like me. My mom is named Charlotte. My favrit sports are baseball and fishing. Once I caught a pike on Lake Michigan.
Sincerely,
your fan
Billy Myers

SOME OF THEM ARE BOLD AS

Sept. 3, 1991

Dear Mr. & Mrs. Berenstain,
Please send me a free
book. I live at 746
Gillespie St.

Signed
Marvin Black)

BRASS!

Some of them are very affectionate.

Dear Stan and Jan Berenstain,

I love, love, love you! xx and I love, love, love your books! x x

♡ ♡

Your fan,
love,
Marcy McDonald

X X + X X X X X

♡ ♡ ♡

SOME OF THEM ARE

Jan. 21, 1972

Dear Mr and Mrs Berenstain

I am writing this letter becaz the teacher made me -

Best wishes
Albert Romano
Grade 2

HONEST TO A FAULT.

SOME OF THEM ARE

March 5, 1964

Dear Mr. + Mrs. Berenstain,

I read your book The Bike Lesson. I liked it. I expresally liked the part where the father got hit by a truck.

Love
Milly Mailer

THOUGHT PROVOKING.

SOME OF THEM
ARE VERY TOUCHING.

May 13 19 89

STAN and JAN,

I am a girl 12 years old and you might think
that I am too old for your books. But I have
been readding them since I was little. Sometimes when I have a bad day at school I go upto
my room and get out all my old bear books and read
them. It taks me back to when I was little and
makes me feel better.

Your friend

Ellen Stewart

Some of them are eight pages long. Some of them are eight pages long. Some of them are eight pages long. Some of them are eight pages long. Some of them are eight pages long. Some of them are eight pages long. Some of them are eight pages long.Some of them are eight pages long. Some of them are eight pages long.Some of them are eight pages long. Some of them are eight pages long. Some of them are eight pages long. Some of them are eight pages long. Some of them are eight pages long. Some of them are eight pages long. Some of them are eight pages long. Some of them are eight pages long. Some of them are eight pages long. Some of them are eight pages long. Some of them are eight pages long. Some of them are eight pages long. Some of them are eight pages long. Some of them are eight pages long. Some of them are eight pages long. Some of them are eight pages long. Some of them are eight pages long.Some of them are eight pages long. Some of them are eight pages long.

SOME OF THEM
ARE EIGHT PAGES LONG

Some of them are eight pages long. Some of them are eight pages long. Some of them are eight pages long. Some of them are eight pages long. Some of them are eight pages long. Some of them are eight pages long. Some of them are eight pages long. Some of them are eight pages long. Some of them are eight pages long. Some of them are eight pages long. Some of them are eight pages long. Some of them are eight pages long. Some of them are eight pages long. Some of them are eight pages long. Some of them are eight pages long. Some of them are eight pages long. Some of them are eight pages long.Some of them are eight pages long. Some of them are eight pages long. Some of them are eight pages

Dear Stan and Jan
Berenstain,
My name is Gwen
and I have been
reading your books
forever. My favor
ite charcter is
Sister Bear. I
like her becaus
she is a girl
like me. My sec-
ond favorit charcter

Some them
are hard to read
without clouding up.

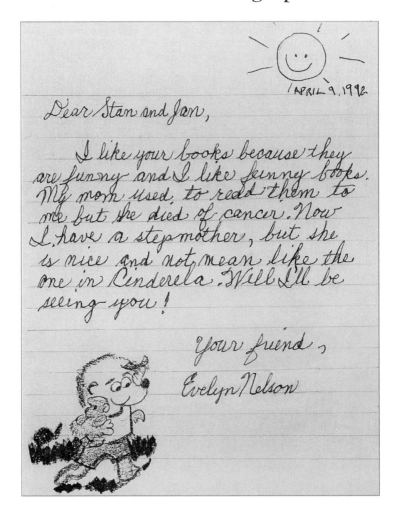

APRIL 9, 1992

Dear Stan and Jan,

I like your books because they are funny and I like funny books. My mom used to read them to me but she died of cancer. Now I have a stepmother, but she is nice and not mean like the one in Cinderela. Well I'll be seeing you!

Your friend,
Evelyn Nelson

But all of them are powerfully remindful of something that is easy to forget as we go about the exhausting, enervating, endless job of parenting—that our kids are the best part of us. They are our future and they deserve our best.

Acknowledgments

Our heartfelt thanks to Gerald Harrison, who for more than twenty years has published our children's books, and without whose faith and encouragement this "grown-up" book would never have happened, and to our sons Leo and Michael, the former for help far above and beyond the call of family, and the latter for keeping us up to speed on the behavior of small children.